Third Edition

NEWLYWEDS

The Crucial First Years of Marriage

Basil J. Sherlock
Ingrid K.S. Moller
California State University, Hayward

KENDALL/HUNT PUBLISHING COMPANY
2460 Kerper Boulevard P.O. Box 539 Dubuque, Iowa 52004-0539

Contents

Foreword

Today's newlyweds are heirs of historical changes, one might even say quiet revolutions, which have radically changed their married lives. They are the first generation to encounter the simultaneous impact of the contraceptive revolution (''The Pill''), a resurgent feminist movement (''Women's Lib''), and liberalized divorce laws (''No-Fault Divorce''). The invention of an oral contraceptive in 1955, coupled with a liberalized abortion policy gave them control over their reproductive destiny. They could have children early in the marriage, later, or never. The feminist movement of the seventies promised an end to discrimination against women in all areas of life: equality in marriage, as well as in occupation. The image of the Captive-Housewife has given way to that of 'Superwife,' caricatured here by feminist spokeswoman, Gloria Steinem:

> *"Yes, indeed, you can be a lawyer, accountant, or plumber—as long as you have perfect children and are multi-orgasmic till dawn."*[1]

Finally, modern newlyweds can call upon a more humane and reasonable divorce legislation. Marriages in several states can now be dissolved on the grounds of irreconcilable differences. This new freedom, intended to provide a merciful release from an intolerable marriage, was also seen as unleashing a plague of divorce upon the land. The probability that one out of two marriages would probably end in a divorce was unsettling. Coupled with the fact that the majority of these divorces would separate families with children, the prognosis was even more alarming. Since half of the divorces would occur in the early years of marriage, the newlywed years had become the most crucial stage of the marriage.[2]

Today's newlyweds could exercise more choices and experience a greater sense of freedom in their personal lives than their parents' generation. They were free to marry or not, to marry when they wanted to, to live together before marriage if they chose, to each pursue careers, to have children at a convenient time in their marriage, and to dissolve the marriage if they saw fit to do so. Obviously, such a substantial increase in freedom brought with it a heavy burden of responsibility to make the right choice. Gone were the traditional boundaries and institutional structures that had guided their parents. In their place was an exciting, challenging, and sometimes terrifying, vista of possibilities.

The aim of this book is to describe how newlyweds experienced the first two years of their marriage, and how they came to make the basic decisions which would affect the rest of their lives together. We follow the change in their marriage from its romantic origin to a more inclusive state of intimacy, showing how their energies shift from a preoccupation with each other to a focus on the goals which they will pursue together. We will cover the interwoven patterns in their erotic life, their identities, their lifestyles, and their career pursuits in these early years.

We have found that a time of turmoil and conflict usually occurred quite early in the marriage and preceded a clearer sense of direction and increased intimacy. Sometime during the second year of marriage, most couples had clarified their goals and created a **Marital Timetable** to achieve them. Our newlyweds found themselves choosing between three different marital timetables. They could choose to have children within the first years of marriage, or to postpone children for five or more years, or to remain voluntarily childless. We have named these basic timetables: **Early Nesters, Postponers,** and **Childfree.** Fashioned quite early in the marriage, they represent, in our opinion, the most important choices which newly married couples make, choices which will shape the outlines of their married life. These plans provided the basic framework within which their relationship evolved.

THE NEWLYWED SAMPLE

Our newlyweds had to meet five criteria before they were selected to be interviewed. First, they had never been previously married. Second, they were recently married, i.e. from one week to two years. Third, they were childless and were not pregnant at the time of the interview. Fourth, they were attending, or had attended, an institution of higher learning, and fifth, they volunteered to be interviewed. This purposively-selected sample of newlyweds was obtained with the help of students in our survey research courses. Each student was asked to locate newlyweds who met these criteria within their network of relatives and friends. If the newlywed husband or wife agreed to participate, they were subsequently interviewed, usually by the student who referred them.

At the outset we decided to obtain in-depth information from a sample of volunteers, rather than use mailed questionnaires with a larger, randomly-drawn sample. In the end, we would still have a sample of volunteers, because of the high refusal rate, and the necessity to eliminate those who did not meet our sampling criteria. We decided instead on a sample of referrals who would be interviewed by individuals known to them, and similar to them in age, race and educational background. Our final sample consisted of 96 wives and 71 husbands; 167 newlyweds in all. At the outset, we decided to interview only one of the marital pair: the husband or the wife. By doing so, we were able to increase the number of marriages we could examine. We did, however, interview both spouses in 10% of the cases to see if we could get better information. We did not, and, therefore, stayed with our original plan.

All of our newlyweds were residents of San Francisco Bay Area counties, the majority from Alameda County. They were young, most all in their early to mid-twenties. And they were relatively well-educated. One out of three had Bachelor or higher degrees; and all had been, or still were, attending a college or a university. In sum, they were young, recently married, middle-class Californians; the post war baby-boom generation, coming of age.

The interview was designed to provide a complete life history of the newlywed. It covered their family and childhood experiences, their adolescent years, their youth and early adulthood, their courtship, and their present marital experiences. Finally, every interview was accompanied by a fairly extensive set of observations on the newlywed, their spouse, their residence, and their neighborhood.[3]

Interviews were conducted in the residence of the couple, with the spouse absent or out of hearing range. The entire interview was tape recorded and transcribed verbatim. Usually two or three sessions of three hours each were necessary to complete the interview. Our interviewers were senior-year students majoring in sociology, who had received sixty or more hours of training in interviewing and observational techniques, before they conducted an interview with an actual newlywed.

In addition to our original interview, all of our newlyweds were sent a follow-up questionnaire after they had been married for five years. In this way we could determine if they were indeed following their original timetables and any other important changes in occupation, residence or marital adjustment. Finally it should be noted that our interviews and questionnaires were also independently coded and subjected to statistical analyses. So, if a given finding is reported as significant, it indicates that it is statistically significant at less than the .05 level of probability. In other words, such a finding would occur by chance less than 5% of the time.

In the following chapters, we have the privilege to look at a time of life usually cloaked in privacy: the early years of a marriage. During these early years, a relationship either flourishes or begins to stagnate. It is also during these years that a couple experiences the greatest impetus to begin a family, even if they are not economically, psychologically, or otherwise ready. Certainly these are years not only of great happiness, but also of disillusionment, when many young families are disrupted by a divorce.

Looking out at the millions of stars in our galaxy, we may see them in all stages of development, from young, bright, infant stars, to middle age, yellow-orange stars like our sun, to red giants, and finally to dying white-dwarfs and extinguished, dead stars. So, also, it seems to us that marriages develop in predictable ways and that their destinations are roughly foretold in their early years.

We would like, therefore, to offer the newlyweds of today a map for the journey that lies ahead, in the hope that they will be able to see more clearly down the road they have chosen and that the springtime of their marriage will be followed by the fulfillment of its remaining seasons.

Paths to the Altar

1

"All of us know what it means among ourselves that two people are married to each other: marriage is a union between a man and a woman that is sanctioned by society through the performance of a certain ceremony. It may be said that social recognition is everywhere a characteristic of marriage as a human institution." [1]

Although romantic love is usually considered a private affair, marriage is definitely a public matter as historian Edward Westermarck states in his monumental study of marriage customs. Indeed, marriage appears to be usually regulated by custom and law: "In no human society, is marriage simply the private business of the spouses," finds anthropologist Pierre van den Berghe. [2] Marriage is foremost a social contract, created by taking vows in the presence of religious or legal officials and other witnesses. Since the marriage ceremony lays the groundwork for the construction of a new family unit, it is endowed with a rich array of customs expressing its public significance. From the giving of iron, gold and diamond rings, to the throwing of rice, garters and bridal bouquets; from the wearing of white gowns and veils as symbols of virginity, to the hanging of blood-stained bedsheets as its proof; and from the exchanges of bride price and dowry, to giving of shower and wedding gifts; these customs tell us how each society views marriage.

The Family renders services which are unique and valuable to society. Unique because other institutions do not provide them, and valuable because they are considered to be the bedrock of our private and social existence. The traditional function of the family has been the procreation and rearing of children. By encouraging young adults to marry and have children, society reproduced itself and transmitted one of its most valued institutions, its kinship system, to each new generation. An important contribution of family life is the emotional support it can offer its members. There is compelling evidence that some form of intimate attachment is of crucial importance for the well being of most people. The higher rates of illness, psychopathology, alcoholism and suicide of those who live alone and are otherwise unattached, underscore the importance of durable human bonds. Because of the benefits which it provides, society has a strong interest in keeping its family system intact and functioning. By no means has society relinquished its legal authority over the family; marriage vows, although simple to state, are very binding legal contracts.

In the following pages, we follow the paths to matrimony taken by our sample of young, middle-class newlyweds. Although the majority had a more or less traditional engagement, we will also look at an emerging form of courtship, the live-in engagement.

TRADITIONAL ENGAGEMENTS

Engagement is commonly understood to be a pledge to marry. It consists of a traditional sequence of activities in which a betrothed couple and their families prepare for a wedding. Once a couple select the date of their wedding, they are expected to move steadily towards that destination, unless the engagement is broken. Four out of five of our newlyweds followed this path to matrimony. It was the path which promised that their marriage would be well launched if the prescribed customs were dutifully observed. Without a doubt, it was the path approved by their families and friends. Finally, it was the path aggressively promoted by a multi-billion dollar wedding industry. A clearer view of this march towards matrimony can be attained by looking at the experiences of a typical engaged couple.

Chris and Harry met at a department store where they worked as sales clerks, while attending college: "She was working in the candy department at that time. I used to go up to her and tell her to give me free candy." After a few weeks, they began to go out for drinks after work and to parties given by co-workers. They enjoyed these experiences a good deal, recalled Harry: "Chris was a great party girl." Occasionally they would just do nothing on a date except ". . . walk on the beach and talk." After four months, while discussing the possibility of living together, they decided to become engaged in order not to offend her parents:

"Chris's parents had a big dinner for the announcement. I remember she said that I would have to ask her father first before we could marry. So we had a big formal dinner and everything worked out fine. We went downtown a week later and picked out her engagement ring."

While they were engaged, Chris and Harry often had dinner with her parents:

"They made me feel quite comfortable in their home, and as a result, I liked them a lot. I remember before we got married every Saturday or Sunday night we would make a big batch of punch, so we could find out what one to have for the wedding. We used to get bombed!"

After an engagement of five months Chris and Harry were married in a Catholic ceremony. They had three bridesmaids, a maid of honor, three ushers and a best man. Their catered reception attended by a hundred and fifty guests was paid for by Chris's parents: "They asked us what we basically wanted and then they took it from there. . . ." However, Harry felt that the wedding was ". . . too commercial; everyone has their hand out for a piece of the wedding money." They flew to Matzatlan for their honeymoon, but returned early: "It wasn't the tropical paradise they made it out to be!" recalled Harry. They returned to California and spent another week camping and water skiing: "We had the campground to ourselves, so it was fantastic." At the end, they were eager to return and move into their new apartment.

2

The custom of engagement has been shaped by the hand of history. Church weddings were instituted to make marriage a sacred bond:

"The medieval church tried to encourage a public form of marriage—in facie ecclesiae (at the church door) with priests and witnesses after due time for consideration and for impediments to the marriage to come to light (hence the three weeks calling the bans)."[3]

The intent to marry, the engagement, became a matter requiring public awareness and public acceptance if the union was to be recognized as valid:

"Bans, public announcements of marriage intention, marked a commitment only slightly less binding than matrimony itself. Those who changed their minds afterwards 'mocked the church' and might be fined. They certainly suffered disapproval in the community."[4]

Traditional engagement consists of four related events: The Proposal, Setting the Date, Staging the Wedding, and The Honeymoon.

The Proposal

Discussions about marriage seemed to come up almost spontaneously after the couple had been dating steadily for some time. Usually during the first year, occasions arose when the conversation turned to questions about the direction of the relationship; the couple would talk about sharing their plans for the future, for example. An explicit proposal of marriage was rarely a genuine surprise; it was expected to come at an opportune time and in a romantic setting. The relationship had moved to a stage where it seemed to demand a permanent status. The proposal of a young male accountant illustrates this development:

"We were at the Claremont Hotel having dinner. At this point, we were talking about either getting married or splitting up because we couldn't go on like we were going. I suggested that we should get married. I didn't really propose then, but when we got back to her apartment I proposed."

In keeping with the romanticized atmosphere of courtship, the proposal was often made on special occasions:

"For Christmas, I gave her a fur jacket with an engagement ring in the pocket."

. . . and in special circumstances:

"After dinner in a fancy restaurant, we drove to a hill overlooking the Bay. I proposed to her there."

3

"We spend that day in Sausalito with bread, cheese and wine—the whole bit. We were walking down the beach. I knew it was coming. There were no bells ringing, but I felt at last this is the one."

Proposals were usually followed by the bestowal of a ring, reputably a relic of the custom of bride-price, but today a symbol of the betrothal. These rings, usually diamonds of varying sizes, were often chosen jointly by the couple and were proudly shown to admiring friends regardless of any nagging suspicious that theirs might not be ". . . the heftiest rock on the block."[5] In the eyes of most couples, an engagement without a ring could not be taken too seriously:

"You can't be engaged without a ring. You might feel you could, but your parents wouldn't. You'd feel like a fool! You might as well say, "I'm getting married" and be done with it. Engagement, well, is a ring."[6]

Setting the Date   w-day

Sometime after the proposal was announced to their families, the engaged couple began to seriously plan their wedding. They would agree upon a date and try to reserve it at a given church. Of importance to many couples was the selection of a favorite clergyman. As soon as the date was confirmed, they would begin the arduous task of drawing up guests lists and mailing out wedding announcements. After the announcements were mailed, the couple often felt that they had passed the point-of-no-return in their journey to the altar. Setting the date then, was an act of pivotal importance. While the engagement ring signified an earnest intention to marry, setting the date created a much more definite commitment. It would now become profoundly embarrassing to call off, or even postpone, the wedding. Feeling overwhelmed at times, some confessed to wondering if it might be easier to scrap their plans for a large wedding in favor of a smaller, civil wedding. These temptations were resisted however, because civil weddings were considered unromantic and unmemorable.

To set the date was to set in motion a veritable juggernaut of preparations. To handle them, the advice of experts might be sought. Wedding consultants, such as Diana Bright, strongly advise taking a systematic approach. She enthusiastically promotes her "P E R T system", an acronym for Program Evaluation and Review Technique:

That's a rather fancy name for a basically simple procedure which makes use of giant charts and sometimes computers to schedule everything from sending astronauts to the moon to the construction of high office buildings. If it can work so well for such tremendously involved undertakings, why can't it work for the planning and organizing of weddings?[7]

In the opinion of these self-style authorities, the best weddings are those that are highly planned; nothing of importance should be left to chance:

4

"If you are able to plan with any accuracy, try to establish the dates of your menstrual cycle for the month . . . to avoid tension and blues during your wedding week."[8]

Whatever system of planning was used, then tended to be masterpieces of logistics. According to anthropologist Diane Leonard: ". . . bride's magazines present a wedding countdown that reads like a military operation."[9] Thus, in the space of six months the majority of couples had organized the most elaborate and expensive ceremony of their entire life. The formal, or white, wedding held in church and followed by a reception for a hundred or more guests would require the services of clergy, jewelers, bridal boutiques, beauticians, florists, photographers, caterers, bakers, musicians and others.

The weddings of our newlyweds seemed to fall into two distinct camps: the large, formal, white wedding with a hundred or more guests at the reception, and the small, less formal wedding with twenty to fifty guests. Three out of four couples had the former. In these 'Mega-Weddings' the sheer number of reception guests was of prime importance:

"Super! Really super! It was a big wedding. We had six hundred people! Everyone had a good time. We had a good band, Latin Beat Music. Great food. It was one of the better ones I have ever been to."

Also of significance was the appearance of the bridal party:

"It was a big Catholic wedding. I wore an off-white dress, and had six bridesmaids, two candlelighters and a flower girl."

Just as the diamond engagement ring is considered almost necessary for a proper engagement, the white floor-length gown and veil are thought to be the most appropriate dress for a church wedding. White weddings probably became widespread with the advent of mass-produced wedding apparel:

"Before then, even the well-to-do regarded it as an unjustified extravagance to buy a garment for one day's use only. Brides simply wore the best dress they had, with perhaps a touch of blue."[10]

Regardless of past experience, the bride was expected to display the symbols of sexual innocence. One bride, who objected, expressed her reservations in this way:''

"I told them, 'You know that I'm not innocent so I'm not going to wear a white dress!' I felt like a hypocrite saying, 'Here I am, the pure virgin bride' when I'm not. What really got me thinking about it was that all my friends who had gotten married and were pregnant all wore white dresses. To me it was just so weird; it just didn't seem right."

Large weddings were, in many senses, family affairs, with the bride's family exerting considerable influence on the proceedings. Sometimes the mother of the bride simply took charge, behaving almost as if it were her own wedding. The vicarious pleasure that her mother had was recounted for us by this recent bride:

> ". . . my mother, not having had a formal wedding, felt I was fulfilling her dreams and Jack was fulfilling his mother's wishes, and so we made it very pleasant for both of them. It's the parent's wedding and it's their memories."

The attempts of some mothers to control the wedding calls to mind Philip Wylie's humorous critique of 'Momism':

> "Disguised as good old mom, dear old mom, sweet old mon, your loving mom and so on, she is the bride at every funeral and the corpse at every wedding."[11]

In spite of social pressures to closely follow tradition, some couples were able to express their flair for the individual touch:

> "Our guitarist played the theme from "Annie's Song" as I walked up the aisle."

> "We gave flowers to our parents; even to the minister."

> "Our driver was dressed like a Mafioso and he carried a toy machine gun."

Wedding receptions were fondly remembered by most couples, often more than the wedding ceremony itself. While an atmosphere of formality characterized the wedding, the hallmark of the reception was exuberant conviviality. Newlyweds were relieved to descend from the pedestal of ceremony into the warm embraces of their families and the congratulations of their guests. Couples recalled enjoying their receptions enormously. They were sorry to leave them, regretting that they could not ". . . meet and greet everyone who came." For their part, most of the guests would probably agree with the sentiment expressed by one of Marcia Seligson's informants that ". . . no matter how short the marriage lasts, the wedding is a beautiful thing."[12]

The Honeymoon

Compared to its reputed origins as an escape from the outraged family of the abducted maiden, lasting for the length of one lunar cycle; modern honeymoons are brief affairs. For most of our couples, it could be described as the purchase of maximum fantasy for a minimum expenditure of time and money. The honeymoon reflected the need to economize after the substantial expenses of the wedding and reception; 15% had no honeymoon at all, while 56% spent theirs entirely within the state. The coastal resorts, especially in the Monterey-Carmel area, the Redwoods, Yosemite and Lake Tahoe were preferred destinations. Las Vegas, and Reno, lying just over the California border, offered the synthetic glamour of gambling casinos and plush hotels. Disneyland, touted as 'America's favorite playground,' beckoned to still others. The Hawaiian Islands or the seaside resorts of Mexico were also favored destinations for those with more money and time to spend. Our newlyweds preferred these resort locales where they could relax in an unpressured holiday atmosphere:

"We had nobody to answer to. Nothing to worry about. We did everything we wanted to do, and we had all of the time in the world to be together."

Honeymoon resorts offered the opportunity to revel in pampered luxury complete with king-sized beds, heart-shaped bathtubs, abundant mirrors, fireplaces and champagne-stocked refrigerators. "Come be a Sensuous Couple. . . ." invites the management of one resort which promised that one could:

"Dive into devilish delight in your very own indoor swimming pool completely surrounded by mirrored walls that reflect your every fantasy."[13]

In contrast to the well-planned wedding, where little was left to chance, honeymoons usually contained a few surprises. Our honeymooners were not exempt from problems which beset even experienced travelers. They hadn't anticipated the possibility of missed planes, automotive breakdowns, lost luggage, misplaced keys, inclement weather, and disenchanting accommodations. Some experienced disconcerting attacks of flu, traveler's diarrhea, 'honeymoonitis', and other stress-related illnesses. Naturally, they felt somewhat disoriented and even disillusioned when these unpleasant surprises occurred. One husband, for example, candidly described an unexpected snag in their well-laid plans for the honeymoon night:

"It was good! It was neat! I bought an M.G. and we split, with the top down. It was a summer night and here we are driving our new car. We stayed in Sacramento at the Holiday Inn for our first night. It was opening night! I locked myself out of the room. I went to get something out of the car. When I got back, I didn't have my motel room keys. Linda was in the shower at that time expecting me to be lying in the bed when she came out of the bathroom in her negligee. She came out alright, but I wasn't in bed. I was out there in the cold. Man! But it was a grand opening! Got down to it. It never happened to us before, you know, virgin-type thing."

LIVE-IN ENGAGEMENTS

Compared to traditional engagement, premarital cohabitation or live-in engagements were essentially private, and even covert, arrangements. In the first place, the couple felt that their living arrangements were their own choice. Also, they wanted to avoid upsetting their parents unnecessarily. The following example illustrates these concerns:

Sharon, a graduate student of microbiology, met Alan, a third-year law student, at a New Year's party given by mutual friends. "I was attracted to his different and exciting views of life. We were both feeling a lull in our lives and waiting for something to happen." After dating steadily for two months, they decided to move in together: "We were spending so much time together anyways." A few months later, her parents discovered the situation when they paid her a surprise visit one weekend:

"My father even threatened Alan and my mother made several nasty phone calls. Eventually, I was almost forced to disown them!"

In spite of these pressures, Sharon and Alan lived together for another five months before they married. They held the wedding in their favorite park. The wedding party and guests were dressed in Renaissance costumes.

"It was our wedding. We paid for it ourselves and we wanted to do what we wanted."

Professor Jan Trost, a Swedish authority on cohabitation, finds it to be a widespread occurrence: "Cohabitation under more or less marriage-like conditions, but without a formal marriage, has probably existed in all kinds of cultures and to varying degrees."[14] For example, one variety called 'handfasting' was practiced in eighteenth century Scotland:

"At that fair, it was the custom for unmarried persons of both sexes to choose a companion according to their liking with whom they were to live till that time next year. This was called handfasting, or hand-in-fist. If they were pleased with each other at the end of that time, they continued together for life. If not, they separated and were free to make another choice."[15]

Similar as a way to test compatibility, but of much shorter duration, was a Japanese custom, *Mikka kasei,* or three-day rent marriage:

". . . the bride escorted by her party and the go-between stayed for three days at the bridegroom's house. If the young people liked each other, a formal marriage might follow, or the couple merely continued to live together, but the whole experiment was arranged with such delicacy and tact that it could be quietly dropped without the least embarrassment to either party."[16]

In recent years, the growth of cohabitation among college students, led researchers L. F. Henze and J. W. Hudson to conclude that:

". . . cohabitation patterns on college campuses are in the nineteen seventies what dating patterns were in the nineteen twenties—an expanding dimension of the courtship process."[17]

Recent U.S. census data support this conclusion. Cohabitation has increased not only among college students and other young adults, but also among the formerly married. In the opinion of Princeton demographer, Charles Westhoff: "It appears certain that cohabitation will become more popular in the near future."[18]

Most of our thirty-three cohabiting couples could not readily recall when they made a firm decision to live together. It usually occurred quite gradually. At first, they only stayed together on weekends and then a few additional nights during the week until finally, they were living together most of the time. Usually, the woman continued to rent her former residence for the sake of appearances, feeling that it would be unwise to arouse parental anxieties at the outset. Then, too, she could always return there ". . . if things did not work out." During this time, she would stop by to pick up any messages or mail and perhaps some of her clothes and other necessities.

When the live-in relationship had progressed to the point where it seemed more durable, she usually relinquished her former residence and moved in with her lover. In only two cases did the man move to the woman's residence. Since the relationship was now considered serious, continued secrecy became more of a burden, and in some ways, unnecessary. Even if her parents were not suspicious of her whereabouts, she felt uneasy, fearing that their discovery was only a matter of time. For these and other reasons, the situation was usually disclosed to her parents within a few months.

When they were informed, vehement expressions of disapproval were predictable occurrences: "It just blew them away. My mom became hysterical and started to take Valium!" After they had time to consider matters, they adopted a more pragmatic policy and urged the couple to "make it legal". They would accept the cohabitation if the couple would agree to marry within a reasonable period of time. On balance, they preferred a timely wedding to the prospect of a dishonored daughter.

From this time onwards, twenty-eight couples, four out of five of those who had live-in engagements, experienced various pressures to marry. The strongest and most consistent pressure came from the woman's parents, who advised their daughters to end their liaison unless it gave promise of a timely marriage. The young couple was now faced with a dilemma. They really did not share their parents' concerns and resented their accusations that living together was disreputable at best and immoral, at worst. They wanted the relationship to proceed at its own pace. One young man used this time-honored analogy to plead his case:

"I mean you wouldn't buy a car without driving it around the block. You wouldn't make any major decision without trying it out first. Marriage is the most important decision you ever make in your life. Yet all these people propose that you go through this meaningless little courtship when nobody really is themselves and dive into it without knowledge."

The situation came swiftly to a head. The couple themselves were concerned about the direction they were headed in. They wanted to live together and chose to marry rather than further alienate their families. Although they might have considered a wedding as simply a concession, they nevertheless moved rapidly towards one. However, they were definitely not interested, nor were their parents, in a large, formal wedding:

"The wedding was personal, just between my wife and myself. Neither of us had any desire for a circus. A group of one hundred aren't getting married—just my wife and myself. I think marriage is what you make of it, and what you agree upon. It's not the vows you take. They were written a thousand years ago."

Only six out of thirty-three couples who had a live-in engagement did not experience strong pressure to marry. These couples lived together longer, usually a year or two, before they married. They saw cohabitation as a way to test their long-term compatibility:

"I would advise my own kids to do it. The chances to obtain the same thing without first living together are really minimal."

Both cohabiting and traditionally engaged couples in our sample tended to marry at the same age: twenty-one and a half years for the women, and twenty-four years for the men. There were some suggestive differences in family background, however. The fathers of cohabitators had more education and often held professional or managerial positions. Also, more of the parents of cohabitors had experienced a divorce or were widowed, indicating a disruption in the original family structure. It was not surprising to learn that cohabitors did not attend church as often as their engaged counterparts, or that they held less conventional views on a wide spectrum of social issues. But the obvious, and we think most crucial, difference was that cohabitors had previously moved away from their parents and were living elsewhere when they met. Pursuing a career or education in another city, they simply had more possibilities to live as they wished.

THE NEW WEDDING

". . . the only requirement of law for a wedding, that is after the license and the blood test, etc., is that the couple announce their intent, a recognized official publicly affirm that intent, and the witnesses sign the papers. Everything else that we've come to associate with the wedding is essentially whip cream."[19]

As Marcia Seligson points out here, a civil wedding is simplicity itself. But it was typically not favored by the great majority of our newlyweds: only 15% of our sample had one. For those who chose a civil wedding, the wedding chapels of Reno or Las Vegas offered the fastest track towards matrimony:

"The hotel called us a minister. He was to arrive at 3:30 P.M. I rushed around and got cake and champagne. Came back, showered and changed. The ceremony lasted ten minutes. We had about twenty to thirty guests. They left finally at 5:30 P.M. and we went to bed. Got up later and went out for dinner and a floor show and did some gambling."

Rejecting the speed and sparse ceremony of the civil wedding on the one hand, and the size and expense of the traditional white wedding on the other hand, many live-in couples chose a third alternative: "The New Wedding." Reverend Khoren Arisian, a Unitarian Minister and author of *The New Wedding,* sees it as an attempt ". . . to present an honest and personal view of human relationships in today's world."[20] "New Weddings" were markedly different in a variety of ways. In the first place, they were considerably smaller. Being smaller, they were less elaborately formal and much less expensive. Rejecting formal wear, "New Wedding" couples were married in apparel ranging from their better suits and dresses to peasant costumes, blue jeans and buckskins. Out-of-door settings such as parks, woods, meadows, hilltops, creeksides and beaches were favored places to hold the ceremony. Receptions were do-it-yourself affairs, often held in family homes, where refreshments were of a homemade variety. Beyond these obvious differences in locale, clothes, and refreshments a somewhat different view of marriage was put forward, as these vows express:

"I want to live with you just as you are. I choose you above all others, to share my life with me, and that is the only evidence there can be that I love you. I want to love you for yourself in the hope you will become all that you can be. I promise to honor this pledge as long as life and faith endure."[21]

PATHS TO THE ALTAR: A COMPARISON

Two different paths to the altar were taken by our couples. One path sanctioned by tradition involved a large formal wedding. It was a path trod by couples, one or both of whom usually lived at home. The other path was less clearly defined. Here the couples lived together, and were swiftly propelled towards marriage by a variety of pressures to legalize their relationship. Which path was a better preparation for married life? This question is easy to raise; but difficult to answer with certainty. Nevertheless, we would like to give our impression of the costs and benefits of each.

The traditional wedding was usually much more expensive than the "New Wedding." We estimate that it cost five to ten times as much; its expenses reckoned in the thousands rather than the hundreds. Typically, it was the large, catered reception at a rented hall or restaurant that made for such an expensive undertaking. The larger the reception, the greater the number of guests, the more costly was the wedding; an interesting exception to the usual benefits of mass production. For example, at a fee of $30 per guest, a reception for fifty people would total a modest $1500, but for a "Mega Wedding-Reception" of two hundred guests, the same services would cost $6,000!

Thus, the average reception accounted for almost one-half of the wedding costs. In contrast, the do-it-yourself "New Wedding" where commercial services were not heavily relied upon was substantially less expensive. Emotional stress, as well as the time and effort of those involved, still was another significant but less tangible cost. From the moment that the date was set to the day of the wedding, the engaged couple was preoccupied with a series of complex preparations punctuated by ". . . arguments, annoyances, crises and commotions."[22] They usually had few opportunities to relax, to enjoy each other's company, or talk seriously about their future.

There are, of course, convincing arguments that wedding traditions help to guide a couple through a major transition in their lives. Traditions are an essential part of the social fabric and it would be a colder and more colorless world without them. However, we wonder on what grounds conspicuously expensive weddings can be justified. These elaborate occasions seem to have more to do with the display of social status than with marriage per se.

Traditionally engaged couples expected to receive a number of important benefits from their weddings. The wedding was to serve as a solid cornerstone for their marriage. It provided an impressive occasion to remember. It garnered social prestige, as well as the approbation of one's family and friends. Most importantly, church weddings were considered the best form of "marriage insurance" wherein one could obtain ". . . a binding, lifelong holy union."[23] However, when we followed couples into the early years of their married life, we saw that the careful observance of wedding rituals did not insure a more rewarding married life. Were there, in fact, important differences between the marriages of the traditionally engaged and the marriages of the formerly cohabiting? To pursue this question, we compared these two groups in terms of marital goals, decision-making, and the amount of marital conflict.[24]

With regard to their lifegoals, 38% of the traditionally engaged could be called *Early Nesters* because they wanted to begin their family within the first few years of marriage. Cohabitors, on the other hand, were much more likely to become *Postponers;* 70% wished to wait at least five years before having children. Cohabitators, it appeared, were giving priority to their educational, career, and even recreational pursuits in the early years of marriage.

Differences in styles of decision-making or marital power, also revealed different views of marriage. Formerly engaged couples usually adopted a traditional division of labor where the key decisions, especially financial ones, were the responsibility of the husband, a breadwinner-and-housewife-marriage. Fifty seven percent were found to have a husband-dominant style and only thirty six percent an egalitarian one. In contrast, the proportions were reversed in the marriages of former cohabitors where 55% were judged egalitarian and 36% were husband dominant. (It is noteworthy that wives were considered as dominant in less than 10% of all the marriages at this stage.) Former cohabitors usually pursued dual-career marriages where both shared financial responsibilities, budget decisions and household chores. For example, one husband, a former cohabitor, whose wife was in dental school, said:

"We are closer than most any couple we know. Neither one of us is really the boss, we just do what each person does best. We don't try to pull any power plays on each other."

With respect to marital conflict, we found that the former cohabitors had somewhat less conflict, but not significantly so. Since some conflict was probably an indication of a healthy relationship, we should not be surprised that neither style of courtship offered an easy recipe for conjugal harmony.

It appears that the two types of courtship were associated with two different views of marriage. Those who were engaged tended to prefer the traditional marriage with the husband as the major source of economic support and the wife as homemaker and future mother. Her occupational involvements became of secondary importance. Former cohabitors, on the other hand, usually preferred a dual-career marriage, and consequently, an egalitarian style of decision making.

The Honeymoon Year — 1st year 2

BECOMING MR. AND MRS. SOMEBODY

As we were shown around the apartments of newlyweds, we could not help but be impressed with the results of their efforts to decorate. Furniture, given or loaned, newly-acquired items, former possessions, shower and wedding gifts were brought together to create a stage with various and sundry props on which the first act of their marital drama would by played out. The living room was the crowning achievement of this stagecraft. It expressed many things: their social aspirations, their leisure preferences, the probable state of their finances, as well as their taste in decor. It was the living room that carried the greatest weight of expressing their new status. And it was living room furniture that received the highest priority.

New furniture was usually purchased on credit from department stores or chain furniture outlets. It was moderately priced, but not very durable and it would probably be necessary to replace this standard package every five to ten years. Our newlyweds faced the dilemma of trying to meet middle-class standards of decor on a very limited budget, called by one husband ". . . the K-Mart solution". Overlayed on this basic structure were decorative items that came closer to reflecting their personal tastes: potted and hanging plants, mobiles, wall hangings, prints and paintings, and most conspicuously, wedding photographs and memorabilia. It was as if they wished a constant reminder of the ceremonial transformation they had just undergone; a road marker indicating the beginning of their marital journey:

> *"The apartment looked like it belonged to a newlywed couple; many of their wedding decorations were still out: photographs, bells, the top of their wedding cake. On a brief tour of their bedroom I noticed a paper cutout placed across one wall stating: "HAPPY ANNIVERSARY—9 MONTHS."*

Symbolic considerations played a large part in the choice of what gifts to display. Wedding gifts were tangible expressions of the high regard that their families and friends held them in. The couple could draw a sense of approval and of supportiveness from family and other well wishers, as anthropologist Diana Leonard, suggests:

> *"When the couple moves into their new household, they are, as it were, surrounded by their kin in that they have all around them objects which they identify as given by a particular person."*[1]

Furnishing their residence, then, gave expression to their new status and their identity as a married pair. Although at times it seemed like they had erected a shrine to conjugal bliss, their home-decorating endeavors also revealed the persistence of former, separate identities:

"He feels that all of his items are worthy of display while she feels that they are only collecting dust. For example, the green and silver Buddha with the cowboy hat is constantly being put away by Valerie and then redisplayed by her husband, but always in very subtle ways."

In another case, the wife resented her husband's insistence on providing ". . . a flop-house for his friends":

"There was also a bed in the living room that took up a great deal of room. It was covered with an Indian print bedspread. Gene decided that this was 'necessary' over several heated arguments. It would remain for his friends, so they would have a place to stay when they came to visit him."

It would be hard to overestimate the significance that taking residence had for the newly-married pair. The decision to locate in a certain neighborhood suggested lifestyle preferences. The distances traveled between their residence and their jobs, schools and relatives told us something about their priorities in life. Their household decor provided us with vivid images of their identities, separate and shared. For it was in their mode of furnishing their residence that we saw the first visible product of their quest for a shared identity: "Yours" and "Mine" were becoming "Ours."

Most newlyweds would be surprised if they were told that they will give up several friendships during the first year. Yet, couple after couple selectively shed some former friends, especially carefree bachelors who do not readily fit into their new life. And surprisingly, they did not hasten to replace them with new friendships:

"I have definitely matured. I don't make friends as easily as I used to. Before I formed myself to their image. I just don't do that anymore."

They were more discriminating in their choice of friends and less tolerant of lifestyles that differ from theirs:

"Then there was Theresa that I grew up with. As soon as I got married, she started rubbing me the wrong way. She came over and said things like 'Wow, Evelyn, now you've lost your independence.' So that was the end of Theresa!"

The process was reciprocal. Single friends fulled away from the newlyweds and vice versa. The newlywed, however, was more likely to initiate the withdrawal:

"And my friends, my single friends; I really shy away from them now. I went back a few months ago to see my parents and I saw one of my old girlfriends. She really changed a lot. She used to be happy, but she is pessimistic now and kind of negative. She is very defensive." This respondent, a young wife of eight months, added, *"I have kind of disassociated myself from my single friends. I really don't care anymore!"*

Obviously, they were busy: going to work or studying at the university, dealing with the decisions involved in setting up an apartment, working out a budget, and so on. However, these expenditures of time and energy were not the major reason for their withdrawal from their friends and relatives. To establish their identity as a couple, to build stronger bonds of intimacy, required a great deal of emotional investment, like an inferno that consumed oxygen from its surroundings. This time of social withdrawal, found in all status passages, helped to establish their new identity as married partners.[2]

Consistent with this distancing from former friends was a posture of staying out of neighborhood and community involvements. A noteworthy example occurred at an apartment complex where the writers lived. As the construction of new apartment houses ground to a halt and brought with it a shortage of rentals, there simply were few places to move to if one was dissatisfied. The heavy spring rains threatened to wash out the foundation of the access road and the guest parking lot became an obstacle course of potholes. Although the rents rose rapidly, maintenance of the buildings, grounds, appliances, and carpeting was "deferred." Most disturbing in this familiar litany of tenant woes was an increase in burglaries. Almost every week, one heard of apartments or automobiles that were burglarized. Faced with these problems, some residents decided to form an association of tenants. Newsletters and petitions were circulated and a neighborhood alert system was developed to watch apartments and cars.

Young married tenants, with a few exceptions, were singularly disinterested in this grass roots action. They were loathe to come to tenant meetings or even to sign moderately worded petitions. They preferred to remain detached: "If you don't like it here, you should move." A group of five young married couples who socialized with one another did, in fact, become aroused when an expensive sports car of one was vandalized. The owner and a few of his friends vowed to form an armed patrol: "We'll blow their fucking asses off if we catch them fucking around!" (Fortunately, this threat of vigilante justice was never put into action.) Since many believed, or at least hoped, that they would soon move out and buy a house, they saw little reason to participate. When they moved away, it was often without farewell gestures, like nomads who simply folded their tents and left at dawn.

Movement towards limiting involvements and restructuring relationships also occurred with their families. Here we found some striking differences, however. Some newlyweds retaining intense attachments to their families, visiting and calling them frequently. They sought various kinds of help from their parents. These couples were usually interested in beginning their own family as soon as financial circumstances were at all favorable and were encouraged in this by their parents, who looked forward to becoming grandparents. Other young couples used the change of status to pull away from their parents, often choosing to live in another locality. With these couples, the visits were confined to occasional weekends and holidays. They used their busy schedules as the rationale for putting distance between themselves and their families. Their round of activities left little time for sustained involvement with outsiders.

During the first year of marriage newlyweds strove to create a common identity. They had taken on a new legal, and therefore, social and economic commitment. Two areas of newlywed life expressed this dramatic adoption of a new identity and all that it entailed.

First Area

Finding and furnishing a new residence provided a venture in integrating their tastes, their lifestyles, and their personal lives. Cooperating in these efforts, they created an agreeable living environment for themselves and their guests. Integrating the furniture and possessions which they brought with them, with new items such as wedding gifts created a message telling themselves and their family, friends, and visitors, who they are: ''Mr. and Mrs. Somebody.''

Second Area

Romantic withdrawal, the restructuring of their social lives, was the other manifestation of this identity-building process. As they loosened their ties with the family, they became closer to each other. Moreover, their involvement with single friends became less important to them. Sometimes this inward pull was so strong that they became an encapsulated pair in the eyes of their friends and families. Yet, these two occurrences, establishing a new residence and rearranging their social life were crucial in creating a surer, although still incomplete, sense of married identity.

ghost

THE SPECTRE OF SEXUAL BURN-OUT

The beginning of many of these marriages had several features in common: they were searching; either their present relationship was not satisfactory or they had just left one; they felt somewhat insecure; they met under unusual circumstances; they felt like they were involved in an adventure; and finally, obstacles had to be surmounted to continue the relationship. Risk, novelty and excitement conspired to awaken dormant romantic fantasies. The combination of a special time, a special place, and a special person, combined to produce 'a romance.'[3]

Whereas most relationships were begun on a romantic basis, they generally evolved into a committed love, if they were to endure. The emergence of an enduring marital bond typically began as a romance and gradually ripened into a more encompassing love relationship, a partnership. This generally took place in the first year or so of marriage and was reflected in a less intense, but deeper sexual relationship:

"We had a lot of expectations about marriage; and most of them had been blown! For instance, we thought we would want sex every night, but it has worked out closer to every week. We thought that when we got married, we would somehow feel 'different,' that we would feel married and high; but we don't. We still feel like Eric and Sandy".

As this wife of seven months, a student of journalism, expressed, first marrieds carry a heavy freight of expectations into their marriage; the hope of maintaining the 'honeymoon high' lingered on. It was common to experience somewhat less erotic activity during the first year since work and other practical concerns drained off much time and energy. Sociologist Murray Davis describes some possible outcomes:

". . . if one intimate is sexually aroused while the other just doesn't feel like it, there are three alternatives: the former will remain unsatisfied, the latter will grudgingly submit, or both will abridge their usual program of sexual intercourse. In any event, what's sauce for the goose, is often cinders for the gander."[4]

Newlywed bedrooms could become a marketplace for negotiations over the frequency of sexual relations:

My husband believes that sex is the main thing in a marriage. Every minute he wants to be kissing or something. I don't think that sex is everything. It's only a small part of the marriage relationship."

One wife, who was able to control her husband's ardor, recalled:

"We used to have violent fights about whether or not to make love. But in the last few months, he is coming around to my way. He is starting to realize, Hell, you don't need it every night."

As Sociologist Lillian Rubin relates, a struggle for marital power was often brought into the bedroom:

"Several couples spoke of their early sexual adjustment problems in ways that suggest that the struggle was not over sex, but over power and control. Often in the early years when she wants sex, he's tired. When he wants sex, she's uninterested."[5]

Rigid patterns of making love generated sexual frustrations for some, as a wife of eleven months described:

"He has his definite little role of what he thinks he should do. I think he is too self-centered. As long as he's satisfied, that's fine with him. He's more involved in satisfying himself than enveloping me. It's simply not satisfying for me because I don't have orgasms. I think I've carried some of my hangups from home with me."

When these difficulties were not frankly discussed and efforts were not made to resolve them, their lovemaking became a less rewarding experience:

"They've declined. . . ." *stated one frank, but embarrassed, husband, married eight months. "We engage in sex less often now and it's not very satisfactory. I pre-ejaculate and Marcia has never really climaxed."*

The terminal phase in this process might aptly be called "sexual burnout." Whatever it is known by, it was essentially the virtual cessation of sexual activity between them. Some hoped that the passage of time might break this deadlock:

"There just isn't any sex now. Of course I didn't expect Allison to be good at it since she had no previous experience. But it just got to be a duty on my part, so I said: 'The hell with it!' When she comes around, things will be better."

Many of these couples had fallen victim to an unresolved struggle for power: "Since fighting and sex didn't mix too well, they gave up sex," in the words of Psychiatrist Eric Berne.[6] 'Poor sex' or 'no sex' were spectres that arose quite early in several marriages. Conflict over other matters had a way of spilling over into their sexual relationship. Some husbands and wives played marital games, in which one player controls the other by withholding sexual satisfaction. Sex-as-a-commodity led to a withhold-demand syndrome provoking an escalation of reprisals, and a deepening withdrawal between the pair.[7] A profound loss of enthusiasm persisted and lovemaking became a service, a chore, a duty:

"She doesn't really refuse me, just so casual and submissive and matter-of-fact; it's part of the weekly toilet or the formal etiquette of marriage. It's like copulating with a well-tuned, delicate machine. Pretty soon you don't give much of a damn about it yourself."[8]

Why, we may ask, was there a considerable reduction in the quantity and quality of their lovemaking? Why did some couples travel across an arid plateau which, for some, became an erotic desert, from which there was no escape, except in extra-marital affairs or a divorce? Their lack of experience, their shyness in communicating their wishes, their lack of imagination, their refusal to use fantasy to keep their erotic life fresh and interesting their reluctance to try different ways of expressing love, and the loss of the forbidden-fruit atmosphere of lovemaking on dates, were all inhibiting factors.

Some degree of *'erotic entropy'* occurred in most of these new marriages. It was not that romance had fled, but rather that it was transformed. Cooling down of sexual interest was not an unusual occurrence in this first year. Most couples did not quite expect it and were somewhat dismayed. After a while, they accepted it and generally moved on to a satisfying, or at least tolerable, state of affairs. As their sexual desires became less imperative, less preoccupying, their lovemaking often became richer and more satisfying. Shared fantasies, enjoyable foreplay, attention to atmosphere, and sensing their partner's mood, were the means by which some couples achieved pleasure together. They saw that being married allowed them to take more time in lovemaking; to create a safe haven in which to be married lovers.

A likely cause for the rapid evaporation of sexual excitement lay in the overblown expectations that were carried into marriage. Because these expectations were not fulfilled, young marrieds were disappointed. Later, most came to realize that marriage did not guarantee sexual fulfillment, but only an opportunity to achieve it within an ongoing relationship. While the early months of a romance can be likened to a hundred yard dash, the approach required for good marital sex was more like that of marathon runners:

"It's not the passionate attacks it was during the first few months. It has mellowed; it has become longer. It's not just an episode; it's a whole evening."

Most newlyweds mastered the challenges of marital lovemaking. A frank description of this change was given by one husband:

"It getting better now! It was really shitty for a while, though. We were both really tired and never seemed to get much out of it. She was extremely tired from her new job and really raggy and all that. It was a big hassle for a long time, and it made me as horny as hell."

And by this wife who spoke of the barriers that had to be overcome:

"Oh, yeah, it has gotten a lot better. Well, at first we had a lot to learn. Both of us were self-conscious at first. Jim is really not an affectionate person, but now he has become more affectionate—which is nice because I need it. But I am also more secure. I don't need it all of the time like I did when we first got married."

As another woman suggested, enjoyable sexual relations were indeed an achievement for some newlyweds:

"Before I could never have climaxes. Now I can! It just happened a couple of months ago. I am still a little nervous, but it's a lot better. Now we have mutual orgasms all the time, which has become almost routine. We have even talked about it and we know that it's going to be a mutual orgasm."

TAKING CARE OF BUSINESS

The old age adage, "Two can live as cheaply as one," simply did not fit the economic realities of the first year. Financial problems bedeviled those young men and women who had lived under their parents' roof before marriage, where bed and board had been provided more or less freely. Now they faced rent, utility and grocery bills, commuting costs and all the other expenses of living together. A small number would struggle to pay for wedding expenses and other debts incurred when they were single. Most importantly, their plans to acquire new furniture, household appliances, or a second car exerted strong claims, making their paychecks seem woefully inadequate. "The battle of the budget," as one newlywed put it, was often the most formidable external challenge of the first year. Their actual financial situation was not as crucial as their perception of it. They came to see that the first necessity was to control their expenditures, to live within their means. MONEY: who earns it and who spends it, where it comes from, and where it goes was a major conflict in the middle of the first year. Without financial agreements, explicit or tacit, no effective way to handle present necessities would be developed.

At first, their efforts to play the role of wife or husband would not be very polished. The strain of meeting new expectations seemed overwhelming at times. As they fumbled into their respective roles they would not immediately feel comfortable. A great deal of importance was given by newlywed wives to becoming competent homemakers. The praises of husbands, families and admiring friends were much like music to their ears:

"I was a passably good cook before we married. Unfortunately, my repertoire was limited. Now I have the opportunity to prepare a wide variety of dishes and I am surprised that I really enjoy it. Brad does, too. He gained ten pounds!"

But after achieving an acceptable degree of competence, the young wife began to look to her husband for assistance. After experiencing his distaste for cooking and cleaning, she resigned herself to doing most of the housework. The state of affairs was well described by a young English wife, reported by Dr. Ann Oakley in her study on housework:

"He doesn't do anything regularly, but he will do anything occasionally. Well, in theory he will; in practice he doesn't do anything at all!"[9]

With the enormous wave of married women entering the labor force, the sharing of housework became a burning issue for this generation. They wanted to reduce household chores, organize them more efficiently, and, in general, limit their significance. For the first nine months, or so, they would try to master cooking and cleaning but by the end of the first year, many would have lost their zest for domesticity and want to rejoin the outside world. Unless they wanted to stay home and have a child, their originally intense involvement with homemaking began to decline.

For the new husband, the demands of marriage did not appear as abruptly or as distinctly as for their wives. They could now pursue a career, with greater dedication and single-mindedness. 'Home Cooking and Home Loving' more than compensated for their forgone bachelor's freedoms. Marriage gave these young men a sense of personal expansiveness:

"Having resolved the early crisis of what Erikson calls the state of intimacy versus isolation, they are riding on a wave of confidence. One gets the sense of an almost explosive burst of energy as if their newly won independence from parental authority, as symbolized and formalized by their marriage, has prompted a burgeoning outward in many directions."[10]

Contrary to the popular view that matrimony decreases male prerogatives, most newlywed men prospered in marriage: their lives were more organized, their energies more focused, their health seemed better and their mood was more positive. Sharing their lives seemed to help them in many ways. Certainly, in reflective moments, some would wonder if they were really ready to settle down? Nostalgic recollections of their single life never loomed too large for the majority, however.

Still, there was one part of his life that could become problematic: Will he be able to pursue a career that he enjoys and also provides an income that is acceptable? Failing this, he might become defensive and depressed if he measured his worth in terms of his earning power. In our interviews with recently married men, we have listened many times to their wish for a rapid increase in income. One man put it bluntly:

"This job ain't shit! Even if I get to be the manager at—(chain shoe store), we will never have enough to get ahead. As soon as I graduate from college, I'll be heading for greener pastures. You can bet on it!"

Our typical young husband began to turn his energies outward, into his job or career, while his wife was focusing inward on the new marriage, sometimes leading to the feeling that they were passing each other by, like ship in the night. If he was succeeding, he generally believed he was a good husband. If, on the other hand, he was in a dead-end job, his frustration spread into other areas of his life and his wife began to doubt that she had hitched her wagon to a star.

COMMUNICATING CONFLICT

"How was your day at work? Who did you see? What did they say? Yappity Yap! I don't have much patience for small talk."

In the romanticized world of courtship there seemed to be no problem to find interesting matters to talk about. However, as married life settled into a routine, a veil of silence began to drop between some couples, and unspoken conflicts arose. When the interests, views and opinions of each were not shared, when there were few occasions for interaction or rewarding conversation, each felt taken for granted and trapped in an endless round of daily activities: a 'prisoner of wedlock'. Thus for some couples, the first year of marriage revealed an unwillingness to share the other's world. Slightly more than half, 57%, of our sample reported frequent episodes of serious conflict in their first year of marriage. After this peak, usually a few months before and after their first anniversary, the intensity and frequency of their disputes declined.

They found themselves confronting a disconcerting array of surprises, as this exasperated wife expressed:

> *"It's very hard to live with a person, I've found, because you don't know things about him until you live with him. I hate the way Steve gets ready for bed. It drives me nuts! He goes in at the last minute and has to wash his face, brush his teeth, blow his nose and all those little things that take hours. When I go to bed, I go to bed! I'm ready. Not him!"*

They were shocked to learn that unsuspected sensitivities might ignite displays of emotional pyrotechnics:

> *"See that stain on the curtain!"* asked one wife. *"That was a scoop of lemon custard ice cream! How was I to know that he had such a bad day at work? Sometimes it's like walking on eggs around here!"*

Although most preferred to argue in private, some couples actually preferred to have spectators, or at least, auditors, for their theatrical performances, earning them the attention of neighborhood gossips:

> *"Like I'll ask him a question and he won't answer, so I'll end up screaming! We'll have a knock-down-drag-out-fight and I'll race for the car. If I get to the car, he'll pull off the distributor cap and we'll have a big fight right there in the apartment parking lot."*

A few even engaged in 'hand-to-hand' combat':

> *"I was talking with a girlfriend who was helping us move. Kevin said, 'Hurry up, we don't have time to gab now.' I was standing there holding some clothes and he wanted to give me some more. I said, 'If you bitch at me one more time, I am going to punch you in the mouth!' That was it; he threw the car keys at me."*

A fear of losing control seemed to be an underlying issue in several of these early skirmishes. When their paramount concern was living within their means, if one partner was a spendthrift and the other more frugal, the rapid depletion of their income might quickly bring them to loggerheads. Furthermore, if they felt impoverished and their future did not seem much brighter, an escalating series of arguments would begin. This was seen as an especially serious matter by those couples whose first priority was buying a home and raising a family, goals which they fearing might recede into the remote future.

Approximately one in five of our newlyweds had serious conflicts over their parents and in-laws, who were seen as excessively critical and meddling, or, in some cases, insidiously toxic to the relationship. In about one in ten marriages, where the parents had never really approved of the marriage, a state of tension existed between the spouse and their in-laws:

"I can never forgive them for what they said about me. Jack still holds it against my mom for the fuss she kicked up when we told her we were engaged. They treated my parents very badly, like dirt, during our wedding reception."

Finding one's identity, balancing needs to be cared for with a desire for autonomy, achieving a balance of intimacy and distance were problems that were home-grown and carried into the new marriage. These issues resurfaced in the early years of marriage as the young wife and husband transferred their attachments from their families to each other. One revealing example was provided by a couple who had a long series of dinner table quarrels. The wife's feeling of inadequacy was triggered by her finicky husband's distrust of her adventures in cooking:

"I'll say, 'Mike, what do you want for dinner?'' And he won't answer me so I'll take something out of the freezer, and it will be defrosted. Then he says, 'I don't like chicken!' The other night I made an eggplant casserole. I couldn't even look at it. He didn't like it either. He always inspects everything I cook. So I said, 'Mike, quit inspecting the food. I didn't put poison in it!' He goes, 'Well, I always did that at home—it's a habit.' I go, 'SO BREAK THE FUCKING HABIT!' I mean, having some fucking idiot inspect it like the Food and Drug Administration or something!''

These young adults had struggled mightily to become detached from their parents and now feared being submerged in the marriage, of being stifled by the roles of wife or husband: "Now that I am free of them, I don't want to end up being a prisoner of him." Not sure of where their boundaries were, they had anxiety over losing themselves in an intimate relationship:

"There's no doubt in my mind that I will attain exactly what I want. If this marriages hampers me I wouldn't think twice about leaving it. People may get in my way, people like my mother-in-law who wants grandchildren, people like my husband who is trying to push me into the little housewife role. Like, 'What's for dinner tonight, Pat?''

Although a sharp quarrel over replacing the cap on a tube of toothpaste may seem inappropriate, conflicts over eating, sleeping and bathroom habits were fueled by long-standing personality patterns. Resourceful mates learned to engineer solutions rather than attempt to change the other's basic approach to their household. Listen to the words of one wife who was able to reform her untidy husband, as well as increase her own tolerance for the disorder:

"He was an unorganized slob before we married. Now at least he is a well-control-led slob."

OR to this couple's account of deceptions practiced in the interest of keeping peace in the kitchen:

"She rinses the dishes in cold water because she heard in a home economics class that cold water keeps down the suds and makes them go away. My feeling is that it does make the suds go away, but it also leaves a film on the dishes. So she never rinses the dishes in cold water when I'm around, and I never rinse them in warm water when she's around."

However the avoidance of all conflict is not a healthy state of affairs; according to Ralph La Rossa, who studied couples expecting their first child:

"Marriage and the transition to parenthood are not, indeed cannot be, conflict-free. The notion that these experiences are or could be void of conflict may more than anything else be at the root of dissatisfaction and breakdown in marriage and family systems. We may, in effect, be victims of our own ideals."[11]

If the couple agrees not to disagree, they lose the chance to know each other more fully, as we see when we look at the marriage of Jim and Georgia Franklin. They had, perhaps, achieved a stable marriage but had also produced a stagnating relationship. Jim and Georgia Franklin, married for eleven months, live in Silicon Valley, so called because of its concentration of computer firms. Jim, 27, is a computer programmer in the Air Force with the rank of staff-sergeant. Georgia has a clerical position with a computer firm. The Franklins had recently purchased a three bedroom, two-bath California ranch style home in a tract of similar houses. It was freshly painted, but somehow charmless. Notable was the lack of landscaping, trees and grass, except for a small lawn in the front. The living room was furnished with a curved sectional sofa with green-blue and gold upholstery and a matching glass-covered coffee table. A wooden rocking chair completed the furnishing here. The family room, adjacent to the kitchen, carpeted in red, was furnished with a tan-patterned upholstered sofa and love seat. Jim's easy chair of black vinyl was placed in front of a large color television set. Above the fireplace were shelves with wedding mementos and photographs depicting the Franklins as children, as youth, during their courtship and on the day of their wedding.

At this point, the Franklins were not well acquainted with their neighbors. Jim saw them as ". . . cold and distant, like all Californians," but admits that he had done little to become better acquainted. Each had a separate circle of friends. Jim socialized with his service buddies, and Georgia with the women at work. There was minimal contact with their families. Georgia's lived in Idaho, and Jim's mother lived in a nearby metro-politan area. They saw her every few weeks. Apparently, they had little social contact outside of their jobs.

Although computer programming offered strong possibilities for career advance-ment, Jim Franklin did not express much interest. From time to time, he did consider returning to college to earn a Bachelor's Degree in computer science. But he was dis-couraged by the effort it would require, although the Air Force would support him and would commission him as an officer upon completion. He recalls the fate of a friend, Greg:

"Hell, he was the most happy-go-lucky guy you'd want to meet. Now that he's mar-ried, he has lots of goals but he isn't too happy."

So Jim remained in limbo, desiring higher status and higher pay, but reluctant to embark on a career which involved becoming a student again. His wife tried to nudge him out of his passivity:

"Go ahead and do what you want, but remember, I would like to be a Major's wife."

Jim was interested in having children as soon as possible. He hoped that children might bring them closer and give them something to share:

"Sure we own this house, but we will sell it someday. Kids are yours forever. Our two dogs are like children to us. They provide a lot of enjoyment for us."

He admitted that he was afraid to lose Georgia; she seemed much less enchanted with the marriage than he. He recalled his anxieties before they married, his concern lest the relationship dissolve into boredom:

"We wanted to get married right away, before we changed and found out that we didn't really like each other. We were afraid we might get tired of each other. So why wait a year?"

It is not a divorce he feared, but the implication that he failed, that he was somehow inadequate. He wondered if his service buddies would draw the wrong conclusions if his wife did not become pregnant soon.

"What's the matter?' they'd say. "Aren't you two getting along or something?"

At this point, there was a noticeable quality of stagnation in their day-to-day inter-action. In their attempt to create a congenial, and workable relationship, they had become conflict-avoiders, and thus communication-avoiders. Although recently married, the vitality seems to have seeped out of their married life:

> *"When I get home, Georgia is in the kitchen making dinner. I kiss her and go into the family room to play with the dogs because they have been in the garage all day and are lonely. Then I turn on the television and wait for dinner. During dinner we watch television. I know this is bad manners, but sometimes I just don't have anything to say. She complains that I never tell her anything, but again, I don't ask her anything either. I just can't get behind small talk (here he mimics a high pitched falsetto:) 'How was your day at work? Who did you see? What did they say? Yappity Yap . . .' After dinner we also watch T.V. She falls asleep on the couch and another night ends. In the morning she gets up before me, eats her breakfast, and then leaves for work. I call her at work about ten A.M. ever day. We don't really have much to say because we haven't done anything. She says, 'If you don't have anything to say, say good-bye!'' . . . so I do. Then we come home from work and it starts all over again, another day gone. Children would be a unifying factor, give us something in common. (somewhat sadly): We don't have much in common now. Before we were married, when we were going together, all of the things we did were happy things. Now all the things are not happy."*

REPRISE: THE HONEYMOON YEAR

The first year of marriage is generally considered to be a continuation of the honeymoon. Descriptions of the newlywed years suggest that marital satisfaction is highest at the outset.[12] Social Psychologist, Angus Cambell, reports ". . . the best of all possible worlds for most Americans is to be newly married and not have children."[13] Or, for example, the author of a leading marriage text who writes "Our comments about the newlywed marriage will be short and sweet. Both words describe this stage accurately."[14] The ecstatic lovers are bathed in romantic bliss, occasionally disrupted by fits of jealousy, lovers' spats, burnt meals, and budgetary backsliding. They are moving forward on the road to fulfillment, experiencing only minor delays and petty frustrations. If they are truly in love, they will be able to work out their problems, and look beyond the faults and limitations of the other. Each will strive to please the other, to be the best possible husband or wife. Further elaboration would not essentially alter these mythic images of the honeymoon year.

In contrast, our interviews revealed a vista of greater emotional complexity. Most of the first year marrieds were surprised to discover it was difficult to merge their lives. They were not prepared for the lightning flashes of annoyance and the thunderstorms of anger. Vehement arguments called the very existence of the marriage into question. Some began to wonder aloud if they had married the wrong person and were stuck to make the best out of a bad bargain. Even the happiest couples were not always well prepared for the problems of deciding where to live, what to buy, and how to organize their lives effectively. "Time, said one wife, is our scarcest commodity. We are so busy we don't have time to really enjoy each other's company!"

At this point a common effort to handle responsibilities was an indication that the marriage was moving forward. Approximately two out of three couples were sharing household chores. Settling on a precise division of responsibility did not seem to be so crucial; the situation was too fluid at this point, and would require a series of renegotiations later in the marriage. A number of important problems had to be quickly handled to move forward. Creating a shared identity, achieving a satisfactory sexual intimacy, adhering to a budget, dividing household responsibilities all contributed to building a more solid relationship. At the same time that they were grounding their relationship, they were becoming more disengaged from their families and friends. These earlier sources of emotional support were being replaced by their spouse's. Looking back over the previous twelve months, from the vantage point of their first wedding anniversary, most of our couples were rather pleased with the distance they had traveled together.

A Year of Decisions – 2ⁿᵈ year 3

Four out of five newlyweds saw a definite improvement in their marital relationship as the second year progressed. Through their efforts to understand each other, they had become much closer. They were reevaluating their past lives, keeping much, but discarding those activities that no longer fit their new identities. Compared with the first-year married, who were intensely involved with each other, there was a pronounced shift to outside interests. More sure of where they stood, they could venture into other domains. Their growing capacity to mobilize resources in the pursuit of their dreams and the construction of a timetable to achieve their goals, is the story of this chapter. To begin, let's meet a second-year couple, the Phillips.

Susan Phillips was a fresh-faced young woman with sandy brown hair worn in a page boy cut. Five days a week she wore the functional jacket-blouse-skirt combinations, "her uniform" as a teacher of arts and crafts in a suburban high school. Dave, her husband, was a sales representative for a dental supply company. He had applied for admission to dental school, but was rejected, and was now taking evening courses at a nearby university towards an M.B.A. His stocky appearance gave the impression of determination.

Their apartment was carefully furnished and several of Susan's paintings were on the walls. Although the apartment complex was pleasant enough, the Phillips were thinking of moving out. They were trying to save enough for a down payment for a house, but were set back in their budgetary schedule by occasional splurges. They had talked at length about where they would relocate: "We don't want to live in Oakland because it's too congested and we are not interested in Pleasanton because it's too close to our parents."

Before they met, Susan had spent a year in Europe as an art student. But she decided to forego a career as a painter after returning to the United States and beginning teaching:

> *"Most women my age like to be completely free, completely independent and just completely, fantastically successful. Just everything they want to be; but what they can't really become. As long as they are in school, there is still the hope that they can get there."*

Now after three years of teaching high school and married to Dave, she seemed involved in building a life together:

"Our lives are really getting meshed together. It's getting better all the time. Just having the past days cement the bond between you a little bit stronger by what you did together. Our relationship has changed, she added, in that it's become a lot more deep, a lot more serious."

At this point, their plans seemed to be working out well. She would continue teaching while Dave worked towards an M.B.A. After he was along in his career, they would be able to give up her income, at least temporarily, and begin a family. They were beginning to look for a home to buy. When we heard from Susan a few years later, they had bought a remodeled older house. An eight-month-old baby girl was a welcome addition to their lives. In her follow-up questionnaire, Susan wrote:

We were unprepared for the intimate closeness we share, because we have given life. To lie together in the darkness with a newborn baby lying between you, protected in your arms, rhythmically breathing together; an ancient song of life."

THE PURSUIT OF INTIMACY

The residences of our second-year newlyweds gave the distinct impression of settledness. They had acquired more furniture. There were more pictures on the wall, more decorations on the shelves and more carpets on the floors. Living room and dining room ensembles were beginning to appear. Gone was the sparsely furnished, transitory feeling of the apartments of the just married. Their households were more organized and livable. Noteworthy was the adoption of pets by many couples; puppies and kittens provided ". . . the patter of tiny feet." While self-contained acquaria were often the bachelor's companion; second-year couples had moved up to mammals, who were often treated like children:

"I'm feeling more secure now. My husband, me and our two cats are our household. We are beginning to see how we will manage our children by the way we discipline our cats!"

Their daily schedule revolved closely around their jobs and for many their college classes; these demands would keep them busy into the late evenings. At times they felt overburdened, overextended and overwhelmed. On weekends, when they had finished their chores such as laundry and shopping, they visited family or friends, or stayed around the apartment. They simply did not 'party' as avidly as before. Their lives were less frenetic; more settled into a workable rhythm. Not only had their living space and daily schedule taken on a more coherent organization, but the relationship itself showed unmistakable signs of moving to a new stability.

A better organized household was only a stage setting for a more important development. Although the Latin roots of "companionship" (sharing bread) and "comradeship" (sharing rooms) suggest this state of affairs, there may be no more descriptive word in our language for this experience than **Intimacy**. Webster's defines Intimacy as:

". . . belonging to, or characterizing one's deepest nature." Sharing one's deepest nature, then would seem necessary to achieve intimacy.

Less intense concern over control, a truce in the struggle of wills, greater acceptance of limitations, fewer explosive conflicts and finally an enlarged capacity to share dreams of the future, as well as everyday experiences were important changes that appeared in the second year. Changes that bespoke Intimacy.

When we inquired about changes in their relationship, only a few said that ". . . nothing has really changed." The majority deluged us with positive descriptions:

"We've grown together in these last few months."

"We're less insecure. . . ."

"Our relationship is getting more mellow."

". . . more settled and comfortable."

"We are more stable now."

"It's definitely improved. . . ."

"I'm glad we hung in there, we've become much better friends."

These descriptions revealed the emotional distance they had traveled. They had, for example, relaxed the struggle for control:

"Sid and I each wanted our own way. We worked hard to change this. We learned not to be so selfish. If we hadn't changed, we couldn't have continued to live together."

They were less likely to retaliate in a revengeful manner:

"We see that both can't be the boss and we give in a lot more. We don't go out on a rampage and buy stuff we can't afford."

They were able to compromise without losing integrity:

"We yield to the other person's problems now, especially when that problem is really important to them."

There was less concern about a possible loss of identity:

"We had a few problems getting used to each other as persons. The important thing is that we are discussing more now. We are trying to figure out how each feel about different things and encourage each other in this kind of freedom."

They had come to a new perspective on Intimacy:

"First off, my wife and I are good companions in that we relate to where each other is at—anything and everything. I see a lot of people getting married. Sure, they love each other, but they're not friends to each other. It's almost, like you know, one time you're a husband, another time you're a friend with an open ear. That to me is companionship, a good relationship."

As they became more psychologically intimate with one another, they were able to accept some decline in the frequency of their lovemaking:

"I don't think we are as affectionate as we once were, the newness has worn off. But in other respects we are closer, more attuned to each other's needs."

Second-year couples saw sexuality as a part of their total relationship, rather than its exclusive focus:

"I think our definition of Love has changed, said one woman. You know, when you are first married you feel tense, all excited; but a more quiet type of deeper love has come—not the kind of love you see in those x-rated movies. There is more to marriage than that!"

A husband, married twenty months, gave this concise description of the change:

I think we passed through the stage, "Well, we are living together and it's cool." Now we are much more intimate, and I love her that much more. I enjoy her more and I get more fulfillment from our life together."

Human relationships, like the people who comprise them, have a past, a present and an anticipated future. Only brief, but intense relationships, short love affairs, for example, seem to exist only in the present. For an enduring relationship, we have to take thought of its future. And second-year couples were, indeed, more future-oriented. The first year had tested their commitment. Their efforts at communication had begun to show results. The ship of matrimony was sailing in a new direction: **the future.**

LIVING TOGETHER

According to marriage counselor, Daniel Goldstein, the first stage of marriage ". . . is characterized by openness, optimism and mutual engrossment. It's wonderful, but it doesn't last."[1] "Income and In-Laws," or "Cash Flow and Kin", are capsule descriptions of the most probable conflicts. The distance between their limited incomes and their expanding expenses set the stage for the well-known " . . . battle of the budget." Conflicts over in-laws, and to some extent, old friends, flared up because of the influence which these outsiders continued to exert on the new marriage. 'Meddling Mothers-in-Law', as depicted in everyday parlance, sometimes created smoldering problems that persisted throughout the first years. As expected, couples who experienced a high degree of conflict, quite often had parents who themselves had stormy marriages.

Why did the power kegs of money and in-laws produce such explosive arguments in the first year? Perhaps because they were also struggles for a sense of control. Sharing the kitchen, the bedroom, and the bath could become a daily test of one's tolerance for slovenliness and disorder. The merging of their lives and fates brought forth for many a concern for personal boundaries. As a recently divorced wife wrote in her follow-up questionnaire:

> *"My former husband and I created a relationship that was stifling to both of us. We were overly dependent and would not allow enough space to experience ourselves as individuals."*

In retrospect, the arguments of the first year, as discomforting as they were, may have been necessary to achieve a better understanding of the other. After some disenchantment, conflict tended to reduce in intensity and discussion usually shifted to a more focused concern with their life goals. Specifically, should they each pursue careers and postpone a family or should they forego contraceptive precautions and let nature take its course? For those wives who dreamt of having a home and family soon, the delays required to new perspective as this wife stated: "We would all like to have a dream-come-true-life which we can mold to our specifications, but we can't." Career goals won out over the decision to begin a family for most of these middle-class couples. Inadequate incomes, meager savings accounts, a general sense of unreadiness, and a wish to build a stronger marriage were the reasons they gave their careers precedence.

Marital conflict decreased significantly for most couples in the second year. Consequently, all of our measures of marital adjustment showed a sizeable increase. Their efforts to communicate had begun to pay unanticipated benefits:

> *"I've learned what a wonderful thing it is to be honest about myself with others. I take responsibility for my life and I have a fantastic time doing it. The downs are just as great as the ups."*

In the second year, husbands reported significantly higher degrees of satisfaction with their marriages than the wives. The average husband came across as pleased with the marriage. The wives however expressed more reservations. Second-year wives appeared to be waiting for the shape of things to come. At this point, neither could they claim a clear identity in the world of careers, nor in the world of the family. In comparison, the husbands were flourishing. They were, on the whole, healthy, energetic, and optimistic about the future. They rarely cast backward glances at their bachelor days. They expressed little envy for their unmarried friends who, were now sometimes seen as immature. Most couples were not concerned over the loss of some of their romantic illusions. They turned their attention to getting on with their lives:

"I think our marriage has become stronger because we both understand that we are individuals who need time to satisfy our own personal needs and goals."

"We seem to have come a long way in understanding one another not only as spouse and lover, but also as friends and as true individuals."

Honest communication, no longer a cliche, was seen as a basic improvement in their marriage. The words of one husband represent many couples who experienced this change:

". . . the single most important reason is that we can talk things out."

Communication helped to make sense out of the changes they were experiencing:

"Each new stage of life requires a reevaluation. That is why marriage is not a stagnant trip as many of my younger friends seem to think."

Statistical analyses of our data on marital conflict show a sharp and significant increase from the sixth to the twelfth month of marriage. Thereafter, the proportion of severely conflicted relationships decreased considerably. As a result, marital adjustment, as we measured it, increased significantly in the second year. Our newlyweds moved through two distinct, although overlapping, stages in the first few years: a **Romantic Stage** began with courtship and continued well into the first year of marriage. This was followed by a time of problems involving a transition from a present-time perspective to a future-time perspective. Conflict slowly built to a crescendo, was expressed in various ways and reduced sharply after a year and a half. We view this **Transitional Phase** as crucial in determining the future course of the marriage. The strength of the relationship was severely tested during this time. For example, the first seven years of marriage account for half of all divorces, most occurring between the second to fourth year. Considering the time lag, usually a year or two, between an estrangement and a final decree of divorce, it seems clear that marriages are most prone to flounder at the beginning. If they meet the challenge of this transition, they stand a substantially better chance of an enduring relationship, since the divorce rate drops sharply after five years of marriage. A second stage, the **Future-Oriented Stage** usually emerged well along the second year and carried the couple into their future. These marriages began on a romantic theme which was interrupted by the discordant notes of conflict, dramatic or low key, explosive or simply tense. The theme of conflict was resolved and replaced by a new movement, a march towards the future.

THE PURSUIT OF THE DREAM

"After two years, you get more into the things you're going to be doing with your life . . . I guess things are more settled. We're finally getting used to the fact that we're married, and we are getting along and getting by from day to day—to where we are thinking about what we want to do with out lives."

In the second year of married life, many couples expressed a distinct sense of impatience to ". . . get on with our lives." One husband expressed it this way: "I'm in kind of an intersection right now and I am waiting around to get onto the road so that I can jam it in first and let her fly." As the relationship became more stable, the couple began to give serious thought to the future. Their focus shifted from a preoccupation with the relationship, per se, to a focus on its destination. Having committed themselves to making the marriage work, they experienced ". . . a calm sense of direction." According to UCLA Professor of Psychiatry, Roger Gould: "We can invest in the future by working out our problems in a new way with the door to escape closed."[2] But flexibility in pursuit of their goals was necessary if they were to have a sense of progress, as this husband saw it:

"It is important for a person to have a direction, not always the same direction, but a firm direction. It's no sin to change your direction or goal; however, once a particular goal is sought, a person should do what is necessary to get it."

However, one in four couples were having serious difficulties in establishing goals they could commit themselves to. Listen to the complaints of these wives:

"Nothing is clear right now. My husband is always changing his mind. Maybe we should have a child. Maybe we should move to Idaho. Maybe we should stay here. Now he is making plans to sell—(franchised cleaning products). I can't tell how it will work out."

Another wife laid the blame at the door of unemployment:

"My husband is going his way and I'm going mine. We are just not moving in the same direction. I have no explanation for what is happening, but it has only gotten started since he lost his job and started feeling very bad about it."

In another instance of the husband's unemployment after graduating from college, the wife expressed her growing frustration:

"So I told him, What do you do all day when I'm working? Why aren't you at least looking for a job?"

Her anger grew as she told us that he watched television all day:

"He'd better surprise me. He really better! I am getting sick and tired of hearing his excuses."

When the husband was not making any progress, not only did his wife's opinion of him drop, but he also suffered a loss of self-esteem, as told by this young husband, a self-described "college drop-out":

"I've wanted to do so many things, but circumstances have prevented me from focusing my energy on any particular goal. I've lost a good deal of ambition. My now deflated perceptions don't leave me much. I've never really had much drive and that's especially true now since I am working as a delivery man."

Without a sense of direction and some minimal progress, the relationship would begin to stagnate as this wife feared:

"You can't just sit there and live hand-to-mouth forever; it leaves you directionless and can lead to boredom, I think. So if you have something you want, it helps you to make what you do everyday work towards what you really want."

In the absence of shared dreams, their daily life could become a seemingly endless progression, however pleasant, that led nowhere. The couples were moving toward a "devitalized relationship" as described by Ohio State University researchers Cuber and Harroff:

". . . the subjective, emotional dimension of the relationship has become a void. The original zest is gone. There is typically little overt tension or conflict, but the interplay between the pair has become apathetic and lifeless.[3]

Finding their directions, the major development of the second year, took the following course. The couple discussed their dreams and attempted to express them as attainable goals. Finally they organized these goals into a plan which we have called their Marital Timetable. The conversion of dreams into goals and the synthesis of these individuals goals into a martial timetable would give them a plan to follow, and provide a way to gauge their progress. Goals, as we use the concept here, were essentially specifications of "the Dream". The Dream ". . . has the quality of a vision, an imagined possibility that generates excitement and vitality," states Harvard Psychologist Daniel Levinson, author of *The Stages of a Man's Life*"[4] The young adult man in his twenties actively searches for those who can help him realize his dream. He looks for a mentor ". . . a person of greater experience and seniority in the world that the young man is entering."[5] He searches for a special woman who: ". . . helps him to shape and live out the dream: she shares it, believes in him as its hero, gives it her blessing, joins with him on the journey.[6]

THE HUSBAND'S DREAM

In general terms, what do you want out of life?

What goals or objectives do you have for now? . . . for the next five years or so?

Of the goals you've mentioned, which would you say are the most important? The clearest?

Who supports your goals?

What steps have you taken to attain these goals?

What obstacles do you face?

With these and similar questions, we spent the better part of an afternoon or evening trying to obtain a portrait of a newlywed's life goals. Since it was the cornerstone of our interview, we probed our respondents until they sometimes complained of being emptied out. As we listened to their lengthy elaborations, it became apparent that most young husbands had a 'dream of achievement'. They wanted to be rewarded for their efforts, their performance in some area of life. They dreamt of excelling as a student, in a career, or perhaps as an artist or athlete. Middle-class husbands saw occupational achievement as a vehicle for attaining other important goals. It was to become their chief source of adult identity.

"WHAT ARE YOUR GOALS?" Above all, our second-year husbands wanted interesting work, career advancement, a growing and secure income. And they wanted a respected position in their organization, in other words both job security and career mobility. Since they were novices, they saw a long journey between their present situation and their aspirations:

"Goals? Getting accepted into Vet School and becoming a doctor of veterinarian medicine."

"Getting my journeyman's card in Printing."

"Pursuing a career in restaurant managing."

"Finishing my Bachelor's in Accounting and landing a job with a big C.P.A. firm."

To attain a position of status, responsibility and recognition was the essence of their dream:

"I want to get my teeth into some juicy acting roles."

"I want to take the lieutenant exam." (for a fire department)

"I'd like to get a job with a title behind me. I want to be listened to—and heard. It's no fun being at the bottom of the old totem pole!"

Money, specifically a salary that not only met present needs but allowed them to save significant amounts, loomed very large in their plans. "Money is the root of it all!" said one husband who became exasperated at our line of inquiry. Clearly, a well-paying career was the paramount goal of most of our newlywed husbands. For some, the brass ring of success did not seem far beyond their grasp; they hoped to be there in the next few years:

"I am just getting started in real estate. I've sold a half a dozen homes in a few months and I'm really excited with the financial prospects. I like a career which rewards you according to how productive you are."

Not only were they concerned with the amount of their own income, but they were eager to have their wife's contribution to the household budget:

"She's a nurse. She has to work for us to afford this place. And she has to work not only for my peace of mind, but for her own peace of mind. If she sat at home all day, she'd become like her mother who vacuums her home three times a day, a clean freak!"

Others saw their wife's job as a cure for "housewife blues':

"I want my wife to work because she gets bored at home. If she wasn't working, I'm sure our marriage would die."

The main advantage, however, was the greater purchasing power of two incomes:

"Without her paycheck, we would never be able to save enough for a down payment on a home someday."

As they outlined the path to their dream, several expressed dissatisfaction with jobs that offered few possibilities for career growth:

"I'm your local drugstore peon. I don't really do anything. I'm running the liquor department at—(retail drug chain). Thrilling and fun! I make sure that everything is stocked and marked properly and do any customer services related to liquor. I also collect carts like a high school kid should be doing. I hate doing it! That's probably the main reason why I'll quit because I consider the whole aspect of that job demeaning."

Although they felt confident that they would eventually make a good salary, they worried about the financial responsibilities of raising a family. 'Super Dad' might become a self-sacrificing martyr:

"So, okay, we'll get a new house and will have our kids. I can just see all of those monetary demands in the future. I'll probably be 72 years old before I get my first Porsche. I am sure I am going to get fatter and pick up more grey hair."

The anxieties of these men contemplating the years ahead when they would support a family could be readily exploited, as Warren Farrell, author of "The Liberated Man," suggests in his analysis of a television commercial during a Superbowl game:

"A bespectacled, effeminately-portrayed man in a white shirt and tie is pictured in the middle of a football field surrounded by eleven muscular football players in uniform. By mistake, the ball lands in his hands. By mistake he trips his way past the goal line, stumbling haphazardly past each player. His wife is shouting from the stands, "Come on, Hubby, make it for the mortgage." His daughter is shouting, "Come on, Daddy, make it for my college education." The dog is almost pissing on the bleachers at the shock of seeing his effeminate master reaching his goal . . . Daddy is stunned. The male voice-over announcer is not stunned. He has the answer. Daddy is being protected by New York Life Insurance Co. to make it to his goals. N.Y. Life Insurance Co. has spent the entire commercial showing millions of men, a symbol of a daddy who fears not being able to make it to his goal of bringing in the bacon (represented by the football) home (represented by the goal line . . .) who fears he is surrounded by barriers of invulnerable managers and executives represented by the football players, through whom he will only be able to muddle through."[7]

As they looked down the road to their future, they could see themselves bidding farewell to youthful adventures. They had a number of enthusiasms, such as deep sea fishing, karate, scuba diving, motorcycle safaris, and backpacking which they did not want to relinquish. They were loathe to give them up and concentrate exclusively on the breadwinner role. In essence, the dilemma was one of both wanting commitment and not feeling ready to handle work, home ownership and family care. According to Levinson, young men face two opposing tasks:

". . . to explore, to keep options open on the one side and to create a stable life structure 'to make something out of my life' on the other."[8]

Faced with this internal tug of war, many young husbands came to the conclusion that postponement of parenthood might be desirable. These husbands wanted a sense of accomplishment in their careers. Moreover, they sought the good life for themselves and their wives, and they wanted enough time to get a secure footing on a career ladder before they undertook more responsibilities.

THE WIFE'S DREAM

"What do you want out of life?" "What are your long-range goals?" ". . . your present concrete goals?" These were the same issues that we had taken up with the husbands. Motherhood, most assured us, would yield life's greatest satisfaction.

"My goals? Right now I really want a family. I think about it daily."

"Goals? Every two months I want a baby. I guess it's the nesting instinct. Then it goes away."

"My personal reason for having children is that I want a family. A family to grow with and experience things. It would be lonely without them. Another reason is that they would be there to love me when there are no others, I hope. I guess you could say for security."

Most took it for granted that they would have children. It was, they felt, their destiny. They were somewhat surprised when asked what the reasons were:

"Every normal woman wants children, doesn't she?

"Oh, yes, I think it's only natural for most women to want to reproduce. I'm not sure why, though. Maybe it's a social thing."

"If anyone influenced me, it would have to be my mother. She loves children. She's just like a child herself; just bubbly and joyful."

Children, they believed, would create durable bonds, elements of a social network of family, relatives and neighborhood. The wished-for child would be a tangible product of their love for each other:

"It seems like every month that goes by we love each other more and more. When we have a baby, it will be the same only then we can share it with somebody else."

"I think the most satisfying thing will be just seeing Brad hold him, I think he's going to be so overjoyed that he will actually stop people in the street and tell them."

Some hoped that they could make a second passage through their own childhood. They were disappointed with their parents and determined to be an improvement over them:

"I want children. I have the desire to do the job that my parents didn't do. I think that's true for a lot of my generation. Most of my friends didn't have good relationships with their parents. They were given money, but never really wanted at all!"

We were surprised to see that these young wives who had been exposed to a resurgent feminist movement wanted motherhood so avidly. They seemed to have withdrawn their involvement in the outside world and turned it towards the domestic sphere: "What kind of outside interest can you see yourself having in the future?"

"I don't know. I always picture myself doing volunteer work. You know, the Girl Scouts, and the Cub Scouts, being a den mother. I guess I'm just a domestic person."

In their study of life transitions, Professor Marjorie Fiske Lowenthal and her colleagues found that young newlywed wives saw themselves as providers of love and care:

"Newlywed women's stated philosophy of life showed a relative unconcern with personal achievement. An essentially nurturant orientation underlay their responses, the notion of giving oneself to others, first to one's family and secondly to more generalized others. The idea that happiness would follow in the wake of such pursuits tended to be implicit."[9]

For those on an express train to motherhood, there was a noticeable shift away from highly effectively contraceptives, such as The Pill, towards less safe ones, such as spermicidal foam, or the rhythm method. They felt that The Pill was somehow unsafe and blamed it for "causing headaches," "weight gain," "moodiness," "depression," "producing cancer," and "blood clots." Many former users might agree with this woman's response: "They didn't really make me sick. I just got sick and tired of taking them." An accountant's wife explains her decision to let nature take its course:

"Our present contraceptive isn't all that foolproof. When we were sure we weren't ready, I used The Pill. I changed because I was skeptical about staying on them for too long, plus now we are feeling that if I do get pregnant, I'd be pretty happy. We are really ready."

They saw little reason to continue taking stringent precautions. Although they had been careful not to become pregnant before marriage, they now were prone to take risks as Kristin Luker's study *Taking Chances* found:

". . . it is important to realize that pregnancy is more than a biological occurrence; it is an event of immense social significance. It connotes fertility, femininity, adulthood, independence, and a wide variety of other meanings. Thus, the potential payoffs of a pregnancy include being able to take on the attributes and privileges which society assigns to pregnant women."[10]

Newlywed wives, in the first year of marriage, did not express much interest in their jobs, certainly not to the degree that their husbands did. They often saw their jobs as meaningless and demanding. Underlying their comments, we sensed a yearning to leave low status jobs where they performed routine tasks under close supervision. They longed to escape; they had few illusions about finding fulfillment there:

"I hate working at—. I just hate all kinds of office work. So I'm just waiting till I can quit. I really don't have any career expectations other than being a mother."

The job was simply not rewarding enough; it held little chance for advancement:

"I don't expect to go anywhere in my job (much laughter)—except out of it!"

Another told of her concern over the sacrifices that she felt were necessary to climb the ladder of success:

"Well, I used to want to be a career girl. I wanted to work in an exciting field like advertising or be a stewardess. But I didn't want to do it to such an extent that I wouldn't be able to have a family."

They looked forward to a pleasant round of activities that would make up their day at home:

"In a few years we hope to have a home. By that time Brad will have a good job and I'll be a housewife—able to fiddle around the home the way I want to."

They were inpatient at having to postpone their life as a homemaker:

"If my husband could only get a good-paying job, I could stay home. We'll be happy if we can just make it in this world. All we want is a home and children."

Homemaking, they hoped, would allow them to be more creative:

"I'd like to paint and sew. I love to garden; I enjoy cooking fancy meals and I want to do all of these things when I quit work."

Small wonder that homemaking was preferable to the often monotonous, alienating work in the vast army of clerical, sales and service personnel which constitute much of the female labor force. At home, they could be their own boss, determine their own schedule and feel in control of their lives. As they stood on the brink of motherhood, considering when to have a child, some disturbing thoughts arose. They wondered if they were emotionally ready for parental responsibilities:

"Scares the shit out of me. I'd rather just raise a puppy!"

"You not only have to deal with one another's emotions, you have to deal with the kid's emotions at the same time."

The stability of the marriage was another concern. Would this be another splintered family?

"Once a couple has a child they have dedicated eighteen years to raising it. What if the marriage doesn't work? The mother is stuck with raising it alone."

Added to these concerns were more pressing ones about the adequacy of their financial resources. If they had a child now, would they fall into the jaws of debt? They related the problems that some of their friends were having:

"We know a couple where she is working as a dental assistant and he had a management job. She wanted to be a little housewife and stayed out of work for a year. Then she went to work and got pregnant three months later. She was unhappy at work and wanted a family. Now they have their family trip together, but they have no money. They are going through difficult changes in their relationship. The kid needs lots of attention from its Mom and they have no money, so she had to go back to work. Her mother and mother-in-law babysit during the week. Her husband is irritable and she is missing all the cute little things the kid does and is very dissatisfied. They wanted the family thing all at once."

Although they hoped they could stop working soon and begin a family; they came to the view that this was not yet feasible. They realized that getting a foothold in a career offered another route to fulfillment. By the end of the second year, the dreams of having a home and children in the next year or so had become shelved for many. They had become Postponers by default. At first, about 10% but as time went by possibly one in four or five, would decide not to have children:

"Children, I think, take away from the marriage. Instead of just the couple having to adjust to each other, they have the added burden of adjusting to a baby, too."

"As far as the goals of women my age, I see two kinds: One group is into marriage, having children and raising a family. The other group is into realizing themselves. . . . I belong to that group of people. I don't like the idea of living through-or-for anyone."

By the end of the second year, many of those who had not become pregnant had decided on a longer postponement:

"We have been discussing having children lately and there are times when I get pangs to procreate the race and all of that kind of stuff. I think our tendencies are towards not having them. Or if we do, we will have them very late in life. As it looks now, it will be quite a few more years. We enjoy being on our own."

MARITAL TIMETABLES

The information conveyed by our senses, the images presented to our consciousness, when organized by our mental processes reveals a dimension which we know as "Time." This dimension is not directly sensed but inferred through our awareness of change. When we compared the onset, the duration and the end of an event, we apprehend the passage of time. In everyday life, we extract, as it were, the flow of time from

45

out of its context, we make it tangible, we measure and record its passage by various means. Each society attempts to organize the life cycle of its members. There is an appropriate time for youthful exploration, for starting a livelihood, for marriage and for having children. So also, our middle class newlyweds saw themselves following a **"Timetable"**; ". . . a consensus of expectations about when events should occur" as sociologist, Julius Roth, defines it.[11]

In the early months of marriage, almost half the wives were eager to begin a family. Then a surprising development occurred; a sizeable reduction in the proportion of wives who wanted children within the first few years, and a considerable increase in the proportion of wives who planned to postpone parenthood for five years or more. The shift to postponement occurred with the husbands too, but to a less noticeable degree since the majority of men were Postponers. It was the wives who significantly changed their family planning perspectives.

Wives were letting go of the fantasies which held sway in the first year; they were less enamored with the role of housewife. Cooking, cleaning and other homemaking activities lost some of their original interest. Their studies, jobs and their future careers became suddenly interesting again. This shift to postponement of childbearing, an important development in the second year might form the basis for a dual-career-family, first described by two English social scientists, the Rapoports:

"The crucial element in distinguishing the dual-career-family from other forms of family structure is the high commitment of both husband and wife to work on egalitarian basis—and a life plan which involves a relatively full participation and advancement in work."[12]

As we see it, Marital Timetables were their plans to allocate their time, money and other resources to obtaining their goals. A close look at marital timetables reveals that they were essentially compromises between family-planning and career achievement goals. If the former were dominant in the couple's lives, they followed an Early Nester timetable. On the other hand, if career goals were more important, then a Postponer or Childfree timetable usually developed. To clarify: Early Nesters wanted children within the first three years of marriage. Postponers had a longer timetable and planned to have children after five or more years of marriage. Finally, Childfree timetables did not plan for children at all, and usually were the out-growth of repeated postponements.

As we expected, there was more conflict in marriages when they disagreed about the timing of children. This was especially the case if the wife wanted children relatively soon and the husband was less eager or was thought to be without ambition. If, on the other hand, the husband used the time to secure a better income, and provide a higher standard of living for the future family, their wives usually went along with them. Fortunately, individuals with similar views on if-and-when to have children tended to marry each other. We found that the majority of couples were able to agree on substantially the same timetables; with the exception of Childfrees who were sometimes married to Postponer spouses.

Agreement on timetables lessened the uncertainty about the couple's future. Just as arguments decreased in the first year, once a budget and division of household duties was followed, so also the development of timetables reduced conflict in the second and later years of the marriage. Couples who followed timetables communicated better, agreed on a broader spectrum of matters, and had less destructive conflict.

To understand the development of timetables, we must look back to the beginning of the relationship. Couples met, became romantically involved and then seriously committed to each other. They had discussed their life goals in general terms, but had not planned much beyond the wedding and taking residence together. In the first year, their attention was focused on adjusting to each other, handling conflicts and disappointments. As their relationship became more stable, they turned their energies outward, looking for directions. At this stage, they discussed their goals more intently in the light of future possibilities. The resulting timetable provided a way to chart their future and thus strengthened their relationship. Timetables were expressions of the quest for direction; they specified the destination, the route and a series of marker-events that served to create a sense of progress.

The Road to Divorce

4

"Love is an ideal thing, marriage is a real thing. A confusion of the real with the ideal never goes unpunished." Goethe

THE DIVORCE REVOLUTION

"In 1970 California instituted the first law in the Western world to abolish completely any requirement as the basis for marital dissolution. The "no fault" law provided for a divorce upon one party's assertion that: "irreconcilable differences have caused the irremediable breakdown of the marriage."[1]

This change in divorce law became part of what Sociologist Lenore Weitzman named

"The Divorce Revolution": ". . . more people are getting divorced, divorce has become more socially acceptable than every before, and more states have no fault divorce laws."[2]

No-fault divorce legislation was associated with a nationwide rise in divorce. A no-fault divorce no longer required legal grounds such as desertion, cruelty, or adultery. When divorce became less complicated, marriages defined by one or both spouses as "unsatisfactory" might end in a divorce. Since the rate of divorce is projected to be more than half of the marriages in the next decades; the institution of marriage formerly expressed by the vow "to live together till death do you part" may become "as long as your differences are not irreconcilable".[3]

FROM ENGAGEMENT TO THE FIRST ANNIVERSARY

Our study suggests that the first year of marriage is indeed a problematic time for most couples and for some "the beginning of the end". Almost half, 45%, of the couples married six months or less were experiencing substantial conflict. In this chapter we'll explore the role of conflict in the early years of marriage focusing on those married couples, which we believe were experiencing intense conflict and appeared to be moving towards divorce. We focus on forty one couples whose conflicts essentially dominated their relationship. We ask, what forces brought them together and what drove them apart. To gain a clearer picture of the typical Conflict-Dominated marriage, we offer a composite portrait from our interviews and follow-up contacts with Conflict-Dominated couples.

The Honeymoon Is Over

Courtships, including engagements, were usually shorter than the rest of the sample. Initially attracted by appearance, personal charm and an acceptable social status; they discovered that they . . . **"had a lot in common."** After they had dated "about six months", he bought an engagement ring and proposed marriage. They were eager to marry. They knew their parents would be displeased by a non-marital cohabitation. Therefore most had not lived together prior to their wedding. Only eight of forty one had briefly cohabited.

In her study of Conflict-Dominated marriages, Mahmoudian found that most had married after a short acquaintance.[4] For half of the men and a third of the women, this was their "*first love.*" They dated less than a year, and typically had short engagements. One third had none. They did not know their prospective mate for very long, nor very well and could accurately be described as "infatuated". Recalling their courtship, several said that they did not really know the other person very well, but only their best side, ". . . *their dating facade.*" Paradoxically, they were often intrigued by the very differences that would later prove to be problematic. Even if their courtship was stormy and they had intense arguments up to the eve of the wedding, it did not discourage them from taking vows to love, honor and cherish one another as long as they live.

Sexual Relations

"There is nothing worse than being lonely when you are married. You have no one you can talk to, feel close to, or be intimate with. Yet you are married. You can't just pursue a love relationship, you are in "one" already!" (divorced woman)

British writer A. Alvarez, author of "*Life after Marriage: Love in an Age of Divorce*" gives an account of his honeymoon:

"Something was wrong and I already knew it on the first morning when I went downstairs to make a cup of tea while my young wife slept on. The wedding night had not been a success. Which should not come as a surprise since we met only seven weeks before and married in a dream."

Describing the wedding, he explains:

"First we had to go through the ceremony at the registry office, the afternoon party for family, the drunken brawl for friends in the evening, the wedding night, the first unhappy sleep, then the first even unhappier experience of waking up with someone who is still an utter stranger. Although we had no revelations before the marriage, I suppose we expected sex to be all right, on the night, like amateur dramatics. It wasn't; and without anything being said, it seemed unlikely it ever would be. What I was too dumb to understand was that although Great Passions may be possible without actually liking each other, marriages aren't."[5]

Most of the couples we studied were usually sexually intimate before marriage and had married because they believed that they were ". . . *in love.*" **"Intense and frequent"** characterized their sexual relations during courtship and into the first months of the marriage. But for many Conflict-Dominated relationships, both the intensity and frequency of lovemaking decreased substantially before six months had passed:

> *"The marriage ended the day of our wedding! She became distant, cold, and spiteful. I became demanding and selfish."*

In the first year, sexual relations decreased to a marital plateau of . . . *"a few times a week."* A woman who separated from her husband in the first year attributed their infrequent lovemaking to her husband's physical inadequacy rather than to any problems in the relationship:

> *"Before we married we had sex every night, but on our honeymoon only four times! I was depressed, he was losing his stamina."*

It is conventional wisdom that sexual incompatibility is more often a result than a cause of marital dissatisfaction. Most couples in our sample had achieved a harmonious sexual relationship during their courtship and enjoyed their lovemaking. Conflicts that occurred however served to reduce their desire. They were often too busy, too tired and too stressed to have the fulfillment that they had before. In Blumstein and Schwartz's highly regarded study of American couples, they conclude that

> *". . . a good sex life is central to a good overall relationship"*[6] *and ". . . dissatisfaction and fighting about sex is associated with a break up."*[7] *and also that "Husbands and wives who had extramarital sex were more likely to break up whether it happened at the beginning of a marriage or after many years."*[8]

Clearly, the sexual relationship of young married couples can be a barometer of the general satisfaction they experience. For example, sexual dissatisfactions were still seen as a problem by one out of five of our sample of husbands married five years or more, suggesting that sexual relations remain a serious concern for many couples throughout their married life.

Money Management

To see how disagreements over the earning, spending and saving money can sever a relationship, consider the marriage of Roland and Patricia, a hair stylist and a secretary. They had an exhileratingly brief courtship in the company of a large circle of friends with whom they frequently socialized. Money seemed to be abundant, then.

After a few years when Roland's hair styling salon was not generating much income; they began to have serious conflicts over spending money. She longed for a higher standard of living and more resort vacations. He felt that they could no longer afford these luxuries and resented her "*nagging*" him:

> "*She was just not a happy camper. She had a permanent case of P.M.S. and complained all the time! I could not take her implying that I was a failure.*"

She remained convinced that he ". . . *simply lacked ambition.*" A year later, her flaunted affair aboard a cruise ship was **"the decisive event"** that lead to their divorce.

Money was a source of contention, fueled by unrealistic expectations, insufficient funds and the realistic fear of the husband's loss of his job. Some husbands in Conflict-Dominated marriages spent scarce funds on their leisure activities . . ."*he does drugs*", "*He runs around and stays out late.*" They sought an escape from the dreary routine expressed by the bumper sticker on one's pickup truck

> "*It used to be wine, women and song. Now its beer, the old lady and TV*".

Excessive use of drugs or alcohol was cited by several wives as a major dissatisfaction. Several Conflict-Dominated marriages involved young husbands who were frequent users of costly drugs and continued a hedonistic or

> "*. . . play-boy life style.*" "*He can't work for more than two days without getting fired! Probably goes off and gets stoned!*"

Sometimes a husband's job layoff will create serious anxieties and barriers to communication. The budgetary and credit problems that came with the loss of income were hard to cope with. As a result some husbands began to drink, became abusive, or had extramarital affairs. They appeared to be caught in a downward spiral:

> "*After he lost his job, he lost his ambitions. His 'loser friends' were always coming around. I didn't want to get pulled down with him.*"

One young wife who "*partied and used 'recreational drugs'*" ceased when she became pregnant. Her husband, however, continued to party and their lives soon began to diverge markedly. After four years, she left him, took the children and subsequently filed for divorce. Another woman separated after eighteen months, said she was raised

> "*. . . on 'Cinderella Lane' and urged to marry a Prince Charming but I fell in love with a charming bartender, instead. We never had enough money. One morning after sleeping on the floor of a friend's apartment after being evicted for not paying rent, I go: 'What are we going to do about it?' and he goes 'I don't know!' I go 'I do! . . . I am out of here!'*"

The wives in a Conflict-Dominated relationship may have married to make a transition out of the house but were still dependent on their parents for various kinds of support:

"She ran to her folks for every little thing! I finally said: 'If you are not happy—leave! I'm tired of trying to make you happy!' "

Similarly, one woman who filed for divorce after three months of married life, wrote in her follow-up questionnaire:

"I was not in love with the person. I was in love with security."

Newlywed wives who were raised by domineering parents sometimes found themselves with an equally domineering husband:

"Three weeks after we married he told me 'I don't want you to have your girl friends over here any more!'"

One husband of eleven months, living with his wife in a small mobile home behind her mother's house exclaimed:

"Living together is the shits! She is getting to be a real bitch! All she does is eat, sleep and bitch! Finally, I asked her 'When are you going to get off your fat ass and do some work?' "

Several husbands were unable to pursue their choice of a career and did not enjoy their jobs. Their only hope of advancement was a slow climb through the lower ranks to a managerial position and therefore he was resigned to a second-choice occupation to earn a livelihood. He longed for a sense of importance. At least, he would be important to his wife and future family:

I am the boss and she is the bossee!

said one such husband. After they had been married for a few years and their children had begun school, many wives wanted to return to work or school. If their husbands would not accept this change, it might result in a rapidly escalating struggle:

"When he married me, I was still a girl. When I grew up and became a woman who wanted to become his equal; he could not or would not adjust to that change."

"Sex" and "Money" were shorthand expressions for the internal and external issues of the first year. "Sex" might also be about the quality of the affection between

53

the couple and "Money" might be about control, trust and commitment; deeper issues, which take different forms of expression in the second year of married life.[9]

FROM FIRST TO SECOND ANNIVERSARY

Communication

Courtship essentially winds down in transition between the first and the second anniversary. The struggles of the honeymoon stage are subsiding. In the second year at least three out of four of our newlyweds showed substantial increases in marital adjustment and decreases in the level of conflict. The majority of newlyweds felt more committed and more secure. These couples prefer to spend time with each other. They shared basic values and sought a common direction. They were supportive of each other as persons and as partners.

On the other hand, in Conflict-Dominated marriages, communication tended to decrease noticeably. Was reduced communication the cause of marital distress or the result of it? More the latter, we think. Couples chose not to discuss serious problems to avoid an argument. The married couple now on divergent paths see each other only after a long day and a stressful commute home. Each gives their best energy to their respective jobs, studies or homemaking projects. But they do not find enough time to communicate. Some hope that having a child will give them a common purpose and revitalize their relationship. But the arrival of children does not usually resolve the couple's differences. Instead, they remain together for the children's sake.

A frequently noted outcome of their communication blockage was a fierce conflict about housework. They could not agree on a division of household labor that they could comfortably live with. The men expected a traditional role performance; a wife who kept their home acceptably clean and prepared their meals. A former "Superwife" recalls her efforts:

> "I did all the household chores with a smile on my face and a song in my heart. I learned to cook by buying "Cooking for Two". I immediately started on page one and worked my way through the entire book of recipes."

On the other hand, wives felt the husband did not do enough around the apartment or house and a struggle developed as to ". . . **who does what and when**". Wives wanted help, but it was not forthcoming as expressed by the wife of an unemployed man: "Mostly we disagree about what my husband does between 8 A.M. and 5 P.M. while I am at work, because I don't think he does a blasted thing!"

The following account by a divorced wife illustrates several conflicts including sharing household responsibilities:

> "We were crazy about each other and enjoyed passionate nights and days getting to know each other, when we were not fighting that is. We fought the entire time we

were not in bed—over everything: the way I cooked, kept house, looked (gained a pound), the way he wanted his shirts ironed etc. The man thought he had hired a maid! But that was the role I was expected to play and like it!

So why was I annoyed at him? I worked the same eight hour day as he did, fought the same commute traffic he did, but because I only brought home one-fourth of the salary he did, his job was valid, mine was not. That was probably why I was doing all the housework while he sat and read the paper. And that's how it went for the next few years.

My husband still blames Gloria Steinem and the Woman's Movement for the break-up of our marriage. Actually I had always felt that there was something wrong with our marriage, but until the Woman's Movement had not been aware that there were other women out there as repressed and unhappy as I was. I think we knew in our hearts that we were not destined to grow old together because of the huge cultural differences between us. I was really a city girl and he was a country boy. We were both pretty immature emotionally and he was very self-centered on top of that and unwilling to bend. So the older we got the less in love we were, the less able to tolerate each others faults. We really had nothing in common, not even similar tastes in food, drink, music, books, nothing! We had grown apart and were unwilling to accommodate the other partner any longer. The love had died.''

This account of the road to divorce illustrates a process that sociologist Dianne Vaughn, calls

"Uncoupling" "In order to uncouple, two people must disentangle not only their belongings but their identities. In reversal of coupling, the partners redefine themselves both in their own eyes and in the eyes of others as separate entities once again."[10]

Often they denied the seriousness of their problems, did not want to argue: One or both mates were not able to express their needs effectively and had difficulty handling disagreements.''

". . . I stuffed it all in for a time, then it erupted like a volcano".

When a couple have accumulated a substantial body of complaints and discontents, **a decisive event** occurs which serves as the "last straw" signaling to both husband and the wife that an "irremediable breakdown" in the relationship has occurred. For example, the decision to file for a dissolution can be a reaction to disturbing revelations such as this:

"I learned he screwed one of my bridesmaids! A good friend of mine, I thought."

It often took the form of an intense argument, followed by what one woman called: *"Bag-Packing and Door Slamming Night"*. No reconciliation was now acceptable. The process of uncoupling had entered the point-of-no-return. Although the actual breakups were often stormy and painful, both parties usually felt relieved that the conflict was ending.

Sometimes, there was a "**Reconciliation**", a final effort to salvage the marriage. Perhaps there were talks with one or more counselors or concerned others that brought the couple back together for another try. However, these discussions often only confirmed their original decision to separate.

A typical scenario involved a combination of events, of mounting discontents, of attempts to solve the problems, then a final blow-out, or a sad recognition that the relationship was essentially defunct, "irremediably broken" in legal terminology.

Our relationship has deteriorated to the point that I can only stand to be around her or in the same room with her for only a short period of time. (Husband, divorced after four years marriage)

Although they may still love one another, they were not willing to pay the high price of continuing to live together. According to Jackson and Lederer:

"The best reason for a divorce is that the man and wife cannot function together without serious damage to one or both physically or emotionally."[11]

Directionality

Marital conflict rises sharply toward the end of the first year. Our study suggests that the intense, but short-lived conflict phase dealt with important future issues that must be discussed if the couple's relationship is to evolve and move onward. Several wives in Conflict-Dominated marriages complained of their husband's lack of direction:

"I told him I was tired of hearing about his dreams, his little plans about how we were going to be rich when he got this job or that job."

"I said if you really think I should be a housewife, go out and get a second job—and be a real husband!"

Conflict usually continues at a high level well into the second year, then appears to abate rapidly toward the closing months of the second year of marriage. Their efforts to communicate created a sense of partnership. They had developed a common direction, which was operationalized as a marital timetable.

To agree on their timetable, they needed to communicate effectively. At the end of first year, they had either launched a long term partnership or they had reduced their communication and began to have problems. The more strongly bonded couples tended to agree on the direction of their future while the conflicters were still preoccupied with everyday matters. In their work with couples, Jackson and Lederer also found that a sense of direction, of movement towards goals was important for the health of the relationship:

> *"Interviews with hundreds of couples clearly show that those who resign themselves to a static relationship are inviting divorce, desertion or disaster."*[12]

Conflicters could not move on to a consideration of life goals because they were absorbed by the distress and uncertainty of the relationship itself. Educational and career plans were put on hold and not discussed. Even stronger avoidance was shown by the lack of agreement over when to start a family. Many among the Conflict-Dominated unions would not start a family unless other matters were resolved:

> *"Like my mother said, 'I hope you don't have children until you and Michael are going to stay together.' "*

> *"I want to wait five years before deciding about having children because I don't know if I want to spend the rest of my life with her."*

However some Early Nesters felt no hesitations about conceiving a child even if they were quarreling a good deal:

> *"I was getting bored with the 'school-work-home' routine, the excitement of being newlyweds was already kind of wearing off. Having a baby would be fun. I kept thinking once the baby was born, things would change . . ."*

At the end of the second year, husbands moved into a more stable pattern. Their mood was more contented, and optimistic. If they had confidence in their earning capacity or career prospects, they usually felt successful and adequate as the husband. Whereas husbands' satisfaction increased in the second year; the wives' seem to decrease. Although at six months, marital adjustment was considered "good to excellent" for 64% of women, it had dropped to 45% by the end of the second year. Why? Perhaps the choice of parenthood versus a career came up at that time. More than half had disagreements over when or even if, to have a family. Husbands were sometimes more eager than the wives to have a child.

> *"As we see in these postponer wives,"* Mahmoundian states, *"the wife is the one who wishes to be independent through postponing children and pursuing educational and career objectives rather than caring for a household or raising children."*[13]

Starting a family as a major goal became important after the issues of commitment, sharing and sexual intimacy were addressed. The first year was devoted to the Present, to adjustment between hopes and realities, the second year to the Future, to a shared direction. We believe that the question of if-and-when to have a child was the most fundamental agreement to be worked out in the second year. If they could reach an agreement, it would shape the direction and the timetable of their marriage as Early Nesters, Postponers or Childfrees.

CONCLUSIONS

Marriages which came out of the two year period had resolved, at least provisionally, some basic disagreements. Their conflicts and differences could be handled in a more creative way. Their relations would have acquired a procedure for resolving differences, a sort of safety valve. Better communication was an achievement for second year couples. At least three quarters of couples appeared to be moving forward with better communication and, we think, a stronger marriage.

However, it appears that those couples plagued with sexual dissatisfactions and poor communication skills, and also those struggling with differences in money management and marital timetables were more likely to be at a high risk for an early divorce. We also wonder if many of the first year casualties were simply misalliances that were not destined to remain married very long. Psychiatrist Henry V. Dicks suggests why:

"Many tensions and misunderstandings between partners seem to result when the disappointment which one or both of them feel and resent, that the other fails to play the role of spouse after the manner of some stereotype or figure in their fantasy world."[14]

Conflict-Dominated couples had great difficulties resolving their differences and simply getting along. They seem to lack a sense of direction. They had discovered realities about each other and about marriage that were more disconcerting than they ever expected. And it was the loss of their cherished illusions, their fond hopes and their youthful expectations that led them to uncouple, as this divorced woman expressed:

"Its amazing to look back and see all that we accomplished and destroyed in such little time."

Early Nester Couples 5

THE SHEPARDS: AN EARLY NESTER COUPLE

"If he gets a promotion, then I will get the things I want. Mainly a family with four kids, a house with a big yard, two cars, a washer and a dryer and enough money to live comfortably."

In these words, twenty-year old Karen Shepard spoke of her dreams. Karen, a petite blonde, who wore a small, gold cross around her neck, was employed as a part-time bank teller. She spoke favorably of the arrangement:

"Like I can take two hours to make dinner if I want. I don't have to rush home at five o'clock and have dinner ready at five-thirty. Working full time when you are first married is sad; working part-time is hard enough!"

Her husband, Bob, age twenty-five, was a slender, young man who wore his hair appropriately short for his position as an assistant credit manager for a collection agency. Dressed in a chocolate-brown polyester suit, clean shaven and wearing gold-rimmed glasses, he was the very picture of respectability. Having prepared for a career in forestry, he laid it aside ". . . to climb the ladder of retail finance." In their leisure time, Bob and Karen were deeply involved in their church:

"We both sing in the choir, teach Sunday school and belong to the Young Marrieds Group."

Bob and Karen lived in an eighty-unit apartment complex about two miles from the neighborhood where they both grew up. The complex was close to the overhead tracks of a rapid transit system and commuter trains sped past every few minutes. Their furniture had been given to them by their relatives with the exception of a queen-size bed. The living room couch, threadbare and clean, was flanked by two end-tables. On one table, a decoupaged announcement of their wedding and a pair of Bibles rested.

Bob and Karen met when they were both attending evening classes at a community college. Attracted by her long, blonde hair and her diffident manner, he was smitten by love at first sight:

"I knew her sister and I was sitting on a table of old used books for sale and waiting for a night class to start. I said, 'Hi, come here for a second. Who's the good-

looking blonde with you'? She goes, 'That's my sister,' and she introduced us. I talked to her sister the next day and she was saying how Karen didn't have anybody to go to grad night with her and I said 'I'd love to take her.' I thought she was cute anyway, so I called her up and took her out before that night on a double date with her sister. That's when we started dating. I knew after the second date that I was going to marry her.''

Karen told of her reason for letting a romance develop:

"On the third date he asked me to marry him. I didn't believe that he really meant it, and I said, 'Oh, yeah!' I figured if he did mean it I could always fall in love with him later; this way he would stay around for a while. If I didn't fall in love, I could always dump him later. I remember thinking, I don't want to spend the rest of my life alone. Suppose that no one ever asks me?''

They were married a year later in the presence of two hundred guests:

"It was an interesting ceremony, Bob recalled, We faced the audience and the minister stood down below, which was totally different! It was hot that day and I felt like fainting.''

They spent the first night of a weekend honeymoon in a large motel notable for its castle-like facade. The next day they visited Fisherman's Wharf, Chinatown and other tourist attractions of San Francisco. They returned on Monday afternoon to have dinner with her parents and open their wedding presents.

The Shepards were eager to settle into family roles as soon as possible and wanted to build a foundation of economic security. When asked about his idea of the good life, Bob said:

"Well we don't want to starve, we want to be happy. We want the things you need to survive and be happy: food, a home, children, at least that would be happiness to us.''

Although they were willing to wait another year or so to begin a family, they already anticipated their roles as parents. For example, Karen had little interest in any career that might take her out of the home:

"The family will definitely come first, before any kind of job. I really don't want to work; I would prefer to do it the way my mother did.''

Starting a family was seen as just over the horizon; much depended upon Bob's forthcoming promotion. Having ceased taking The Pill, because ''. . . it gave me headaches''; they relied upon a less secure contraceptive for the time being. Children were considered an essential part of ''. . . God's plan for our lives.'' As Bob explained:

"I believe that children are the gifts of God, a sacred trust. To explain that I'd have to go through my whole beliefs and I'd prefer not to."

Karen felt the same:

"We'd like as many kids as we can afford. We'd like at least two of our own and we'd like to adopt two. . . ."

We heard from the Shepards after five years of marriage. They had bought a new three bedroom home in a suburban community, a 35 minute commute to Bob's employment as a retail credit manager. They had a baby daughter and Karen was expecting another child. Although enjoying parenthood, they planned to limit their family to two children ". . . because we will be able to share ourselves better with just two." They had achieved many of their original goals, and were proud of their accomplishments. When we queried about areas of serious disagreement, Karen wrote: "We don't have disagreements." She added a postscript: "We depend upon the Lord for the success of our marriage, and so far He has not let us down."

a family of origin

EARLY NESTERS: A FAMILY PORTRAIT

Sixty-four newlyweds, 38% of the sample, followed Early Nester Timetables. Most of these individuals planned to begin a family within the first two or three years of marriage if at all possible. None wanted to wait more than five years. They also hoped to have their first child before the wife was twenty-five years old. Thus, they were Early Nesters in two senses: "Early" in their twenties and "Early" in their marriage. In keeping with these intentions, less than half regularly took any contraceptive precautions.

Forty of the ninety-six wives were Early Nesters. All had once attended college; and nine had earned a Bachelor's Degree. However, most were no longer attending college. In the space of a year or two, they had become engaged and married, usually before their twenty-first birthday.

Twenty-four of the seventy-one newlywed men had Early Nester Timetables. Eleven worked in blue collar occupations, and eight in service occupations such as police or fire or as salesmen. Two were managers, two were teachers and one was an engineer. While eight had college degrees, only a few of the others still attended. None were full-time students. As a rule, they were the oldest men in our sample, yet were married to the youngest women; women who were usually four or more years younger than they were.

The parents of Early Nesters had achieved their version of 'The American Dream.' They had secure jobs, suburban homes, and relatively large families. Their high fertility rates during the postwar years had earned them the well known designation, 'Baby Boomers,' Three quarters of these families had lived for ten or more years in the San Francisco Bay Area. Most had relatives there, constituting a web of kinship kept alive by frequent contact. Their marriages were remarkably stable, only 18% had been disrupted by separation or divorce.

Usually having only a high school education, the fathers nevertheless earned middle-range incomes. In the expanding economy of the Fifties and Sixties, the family could rely solely upon his paycheck, and still enjoy a middle-class lifestyle. These fathers were steady workers who took pride in being able to raise their families in a suburban environment and help their children to attend college if they wished. Although they were respected for being "hard workers," "good providers" and "responsible men" they were often seen as strict, and even domineering by their children:

"My father was tough, but he was always right. He was right and that was all there was to it."

The mothers of Early Nesters, themselves Early Nesters, were almost all full-time housewives. Only 15% were employed on a full-time basis outside the home; and another 32% worked occasionally. These families shared the belief that a woman's place was at home:

"My Mom was a home body. She never liked to go places by herself, but she loved going with the family. She was a good Mom, always doing things with her girls. She was always home when we came from school and had a snack ready for us."

"Family Togetherness" was more than a slogan; it was a duty:

"My parents were the type that if the kids were not invited, they wouldn't go either. They only left us with a babysitter once!"

Rooted in their homes and jobs, and stable in their marriages, the emotional life of these families was one of intense, inward focus. Their preoccupation with family affairs was captured by historian Phillipe Aries in *Centuries of Childhood:*

"The evolution of the last few centuries has often been presented as a triumph of individualism over social constraints, with the family counted among the latter. But where is the individualism in these modern lives, in which all of the energy of the couple is directed to serving the interest of a deliberately restricted posterity?"[1]

Isolated in suburban neighborhoods, it was easy for these families to segregate work from home, political and economic problems from personal concerns, and the dangers of city life from the security of dormitory communities. The parents of Early Nesters held traditional concepts of masculinity and femininity passed on as self-evident truths grounded in an immutable human nature. Daughters were to be protected from harm and disgrace by a regimen of close supervision. Their activities were monitored, there dates were carefully screened. They were rarely encouraged to become involved in activities that would take them out of the home. They were not allowed enough opportunities to test their abilities, to take risks, to expand their horizons. Most importantly, they were not expected to really prepare for lifelong careers. Dreams of what they might become were not taken too seriously:

"I knew what I didn't want to be, like a stewardess or teacher or a nurse; all of those standard little girl things. I didn't want to be any of them except a mommy. Career-wise, I never had any big ideas."

Thus, for all of their benefits, these families promoted a narrow view of women's possibilities, a view that did not prepare their daughters for a wider range of activities. Instead, they fostered a dependence on others, as family researcher Dr. Lee Rainwater found:

"One of the reasons they marry at an early age is that when they outgrow their status of daughter, they feel somewhat lost and look forward to the clear-cut status of wife and mother as a way of securely establishing themselves as someone again."[2]

LEAVING HOME: FROM THE OLD NEST TO THE NEW ONE

"You know, a girl grows up to be lady who gets to be a wife, and a mother who bakes cupcakes, and stuff, you know."

As this Early Nester wife saw it, the transition to adulthood was swift and simple. High school graduation set the stage for a partial emancipation from parents. It triggered, as it were, a brief war for independence from her parents' close supervision; a war whose major battles were usually fought over dating curfews. On the one hand, the girl sought to extend the boundaries of her world, to regulate her own comings and goings. Her parents, on the other hand, worried lest she go astray. They wanted to protect her from ". . . drinking, drugs, wild parties," and other youthful indiscretions. As her explorations increasingly took her out of the house, her parents redoubled their efforts to enforce restrictions they honestly thought were necessary. They found themselves hard pressed to adjust to the disruptions in their formerly peaceful lives and experienced times of intense turmoil. At times her struggle for emancipation took an outright rebellious turn, as, for example, when she dated men who were clearly unacceptable to her parents:

"In my senior year, I got involved with this other knucklehead. He was a no-good-for-nothing. He still doesn't have a job, from what I've heard. He treated me like dirt. I was stupid, but I liked him. My father didn't like him. They would tell me what a bum he was. He would go to one girl's house and on his way home, he would stop by my house. If we went to an ice cream bar, I would have to pay for it. Finally, I realized what a bum he was."

As they gave up these unpromising boyfriends and became seriously involved with more suitable young men, their parents became less apprehensive. A truce, albeit strained at times, came into being. They came to accept her busy round of social activities in the hope that she would soon be leaving home as a properly married woman. Although the threat to leave home was sometimes vowed, most girls were deeply ambivalent about moving out. On their side, the parents were loathe to let them move away and took suggestions about leaving as a rejection. Both parties were frightened to loosen their old attachments.

Early Nester women gained a new found sense of emancipation in their war for independence. However, it was more a case of 'freedom from' rather than one of 'freedom to' because she lacked the confidence to seriously consider a wider range of options. Romantic involvements were given highest priority, as these three women's recollections suggest:

> "I was too busy being a lady about town, dating a lot, to work towards a college degree. I just took classes when it was convenient for me."

> "What good is a degree these days? I made enough money as a saleslady at . . . before I got married. I was fed up with going to school even before I got engaged."

> "I changed my mind every week as to which career I would pursue. By the time I got out of high school, I really didn't want to go another four years to college, I just wanted to get out of school and get married."

Early Nester men had less anxiety, and less conflict when they detached themselves from their homes. Many had lived away from home for varying lengths of time and had traveled or served in the armed forces. As they grew tired of the single life, they began to search for a mate. They favored, by and large, girls who were domestically inclined rather than career-oriented. According to one interviewer they looked for girls who were:

> ". . . sexually inexperienced, girls who don't use drugs, girls who are not into women's liberation, girls they can bring home to their Moms."

It was no accident that they were able to find these very qualities in the Early Nester women we have just described, women who came from family backgrounds like theirs. It appeared that Early Nester men wanted a homemaker as much as Early Nester Women wanted a home-away-from-home. Early Nester women were looking for a man to support them and Early Nester men were, by and large, ready and willing to do so. For them, marriage was often an exchange of economic support for domestic and sexual service. However, the garb of romantic fantasy usually cloaked the bare bones of this exchange as Nancy Chodorow explains:

"Conventional wisdom has it, and much of our everyday observation confirms, that women are the romantic ones in our society, the ones for whom love and marriage and relationships matter. However, several studies point to ways that men love and fall in love romantically, women, sensibly and rationally. This position suggests that women's apparent romanticism is an emotional and ideological mask for their very real economic dependence."[3]

SETTLING DOWN

Early Nester couples were eager to settle down as soon as possible. "Settling down" meant taking up their roles as husbands and wife, their duties as provider and homemaker, their responsibilities to have and raise children. They embraced a traditional division of labor with its clear separation of male and female activities. His locus of identity was in the outside world; hers within the marriage and the home. They saw the good life largely in terms of family-related satisfactions. Happiness, Security, Contentment, Enjoyment of Life, Good Income and A Healthy Family were the satisfactions that they spoke of. One husband described his goals in these terms:

"My idea of happiness is to be comfortable. I want to be able to provide food, shelter and clothing for my wife and our (future) children. This would give me a rewarding feeling. I want children that are healthy, job security, and a house."

They carried many traditional concepts into their marriage, concepts largely fashioned from observing their parents. He was to be responsible for paying the bills, unless he showed himself unable to do so. And he was allowed to have the final word on important decisions: "She looks up to me to make the decisions, to do everything! Whatever I want, she wants," said one young police officer. Sex differences, they believed, were rooted in a natural order. Masculinity and Femininity were considered as polar opposites. Husbands aspired to be "real men," to have "drive," "grit," "guts," "balls," "macho" and similar qualities. In contrast, they praised their wives for being "girlish," "innocent," "sweet," "helpless," "flighty," "sentimental," "homebodies," "clingers," and other descriptions suggestive of an arrested state of emotional development.

Sexual Equality was a vaguely threatening, unworkable doctrine that held little relevance to their lives. The attitude of a young salesman was typical:

"I believe that a woman belongs in the home if she is married. She might not agree with that, but I just don't like her to be working."

When asked for his opinion of the Women's Liberation Movement, another Early Nester husband responded angrily:

"That doesn't mean shit to me! The black woman has always been liberated. She's carried the load for the black man for centuries. My wife has always been liberated and doesn't go for that white fad."

Some husbands held a code of manhood which exalted their position in the marriage:

"Probably the most important thing for me is to be a successful husband, somebody my family can be proud of. What I mean by a successful husband is that the man of the house must be just that, the head of his house."

For a few, their struggle for male dominance almost became an exercise in sado-maso-chism:

"She gets irritated; I find that amusing. She gets mad at me all of the time; I like that. I like to tease and torment. She is not as smart as I am. If I need to pull something over on her, it's within my capacity."

Early Nester wives often had their own reasons for supporting their husband's claim for leadership. They indeed did rely upon him for economic support and a sense of security. Coming from a tightly controlled home, they were pleased to exchange their parent's controls for their husband's 'leadership'':

"I found that it's easier to be your own person married than your own person at home with your parents."

It seems curious, at first glance, that so many wives seemed to accept this "Big man—Little woman" arrangement; three out of four Early Nester wives saw the husband as "the boss." The reason for this state of affairs may lie in the disinclination of many of these wives to continue working. They were eager to stay home and looked upon fulltime employment without much enthusiasm, almost as equivalent to a life sentence at hard labor:

"As for me, I think that there are a lot of good points to Women's Lib, but I don't want to work like men do. I'm for being taken care of by my husband and not having to share the work load."

Another wife stated:

"I have never considered the possibility that my marriage will not work out, so I really don't worry about getting into a career."

Most Early Nesters wives held jobs that required only minimal entry-level skills, jobs that paid little above the minimum wage, jobs for which they were overqualified and jobs that contributed little to their sense of self-esteem: "My job is so routine it could be done by a trained monkey!" They saw these jobs as a temporary measure until they had children. Essentially, they worked to help pay the bills and to begin a savings account: "We live on his paycheck now and are able to put most of mine in the bank." Wives' earnings were viewed as a temporary supplement to the husband's. They didn't want to threaten their husband's pride by earning as much as he did. Given their employment in low paying jobs, there was little chance of this happening.

Stuck in uninteresting, dead-end jobs, and sensing an erosion of romantic illusions about married life, many of these wives experienced a state of tension, of unfulfillment commonly known as 'boredom.' They were beset with disconcerting spells of listlessness, fatigue and depression. They escaped into the packaged fantasies of television soap operas, glamour magazines and adventures of Hollywood stars and other celebrities who offered to share their personal secrets of keeping romance alive and marriages intact. They regarded their lives as in a holding pattern until they had a home and children to care for. As part of this move toward domesticity, they no longer took such pains with their appearance and no longer cultivated those winsome charms that had won them a husband. Several had begun to put on weight and were swiftly losing their youthful figure. They were no longer as well-groomed as when they were first married; a metamorphosis, noted by Diana Leonard:

". . . many of them had cut their long hair and changed its colour (usually blonde to darker). Others wore less make-up, or had put on weight, or changed their style of dress."[4]

Avoiding conflict was another way in which Early Nesters settled down. Compared to the other couples, their arguments were not as intense or as wide ranging. Given the unequal distribution of power, it was not surprising that Early Nester wives handled their husbands through subtle manipulation rather than frank assertion. Above all, they sought to build a stable foundation for a future family as a National Institute of Mental Health Study found:

". . . these couples value . . . social role satisfactions more than intimate relationships. . . ."[5]

However, in the interests of suppressing disagreements, they risked developing an emotional distance between them as marriage counselor Daniel Beaver warns:

"It's as if they decided to take a thick vault door and slam it closed on their resentments. In most cases, this decision is made at an unconscious level and once that door is closed the husband and wife put increasing energy into maintaining the status quo, or trying to keep the marriage as happy as it was when they first got together. However, their efforts often lead them down a path toward boredom and a particular kind of loneliness."[6]

Early Nesters moved quickly to fill this void as the newness of the marriage wore off. He spent his leisure time fixing cars and watching televised sports, etc. She turned to her family and close friends for companionship. The wish for motherhood began to occupy her thoughts, as Beaver observed:

"One way she can fill the vacuum is by having children. She has been told, and it is true, that having a child will fulfill some of her emotional needs, needs no longer met in her relationship with her husband."[7]

STARTING A FAMILY

Once an almost inevitable occurrence for married women, motherhood itself, as well as the timing and number of children, have all become a choice. Family planning, the decision of it and when to have children, is widely available in an era of effective contraception. Yet, a number of these young couples were rushing down the road to parenthood without giving much consideration to their options. In this regard, noted family sociologist, Jessie Bernard asks:

"Women come in a wide variety of shapes, sizes, colours, talents, temperaments and degrees of motherliness. They come in a wide variety of personalities and with different motivations. They differ in standards and styles. They come from a wide variety of backgrounds. . . . Why is that despite their differences, almost all females want babies"?[8]

Above all, it appears that Early Nester wives wanted to be part of a network of family bonds. They sought to reestablish the nurturant relationships they had experienced in their homes, as this trio of wives expressed:

"I want something I can count on, something dependable."

"My family was a warm, close-knit unit and that's the way I like it. I don't enjoy a lot of people I don't know or things I don't understanding coming at me."

"Like I said before, I've always thought that I wanted a family. . . . I would like to be like my mother and stay home to raise my children and take care of my husband."

Motherhood, they hoped, would complete their identity as an adult woman. By producing children she could reproduce the tie to her mother and her family. She was as strongly identified with them as they were with her, revealing a mother/married-daughter bond known as **The Demeter Bond** after a goddess of fertility.[9] Her children would represent a precious gift to her parents, who now faced an empty nest and would welcome the arrival of their grandchildren. Parental sacrifices would be repaid when they too could proudly display a bumper sticker claiming "Happiness is Being a Grandparent." Thus, the wish to have children was often an expression of a wish for relatedness.

girls tied to their mothers

By her reproductive power, she could forge links which united families, gaining esteem in the eyes of all, as Pat Walker Fine suggests:

"Early Nester women tend to see themselves as extensions of their families of origin and children as a further and natural extension. They delight in the newfound respect they gain from their parents when they marry. They feel they are finally treated as adults which vastly improves and cements their relationship with their parents. They tend to forget the family problems that they once experienced in authoritarian homes and select out the happy occasions of their childhood. Having found a new sense of freedom within marriage they tend to idealize the family and develop a "We will live-happily-ever-after attitude about family life".[10]

Like their mothers, they considered housekeeping as a fulltime occupation for married women with children. They wanted to stay home with their family rather than use child-care facilities or paid babysitters. Early Nester wives wanted to be as dedicated homemakers as their mothers were, as Ann Oakley reports in *The Sociology of Housework:*

"The learning of domesticity by daughters from mothers is a lasting lesson driven home through the psychological identification of mother and daughter."[11]

Working in jobs offering little interest and even less challenge, closely supervised in their place of work, it was no wonder that the career of mother-housewife seemed to offer fulfillment. Psychologist, Edward Pohlman, gives some reasons why staying at home with children may be preferable to outside work:

"Children provide a do-it-yourself, build-your-own-source-of-meaning-at-home, they have an endless capacity to absorb time; they provide at least small challenges, upsets and crises in a culture that may be bored with its sameness, and they provide exceedingly personal interaction in contrast to the impersonality of many other contacts."[12]

Early Nester women wanted children as soon as possible because they had few other plans for their lives, because motherhood was the fastest path to recognition as an adult woman and because they wanted to create enduring bonds with their families and their husbands. To accomplish this, they only had to let nature take its course.

Early Nester husbands were also eager to start a family. Since the bulk of housework and child care would be done by their wives, they did not fear a drastic change in their daily lives. Their reservations were about shouldering the economic support of their new families. Listening to their reasons for wanting children it became apparent that they were often the same ones given by their wives. They, too, wanted strong family bonds.

Having children was an extension of one's ego:

"I'd like four or five kids to carry on my name and my blood."

An obligation to one's family lineage:

"The first one has got to be a boy. I am going to keep on plugging till I get a boy. I don't know why it is, but every married couple wants a boy first. I guess it's to carry on the family name.

An opportunity to pass on traditional sex roles:

"I want to teach my boys how to work with their hands. I want to play sports with them. I know that my wife wants to teach her daughters how to cook and sew. We both feel that is how they should be raised."

A gift to their families:

"Everyone is asking us, 'When are you two going to have kids?' Her Mom feels lonely now that all of her children left home. She can't wait to help Wilma take care of a new baby."

A form of "marriage-glue":

"Children would be a unifying force. We have very little in common now."

And finally an insurance policy against a lonely old age:

"In old age, we'll have our kids looking out for us and grandchildren to look forward to. It's very sad to die alone and lonely."

FIVE YEARS AFTER THE HONEYMOON

What changes took place in the first five years of these marriages? How had their dreams fared? Nineteen Early Nesters, twelve wives and seven husbands, responded to our follow-up survey, providing a partial, but nonetheless revealing, look at these marriages. All but two were still married to their same spouse; two men had been divorced, both were remarried. Almost all had lived up to the prediction of Early Nesters by having or expecting children. Eight of the women already had a child, one had two children, and three others were pregnant. Only one wife hadn't yet conceived, because of her infertility problem: "We're still trying," she wrote us. Four of the seven men were now fathers and another's wife was pregnant. Clearly, Early Nesters were well on their way to reproducing themselves.

However, in spite of their original goal to have a large family before they were thirty, they had moved to a position of 'later and less'. The usual time span from their wedding to the birth of their first child was well over two years, and one third of the couples had waited beyond their third anniversary before becoming parents. They had stretched their original timetables. They had hoped to have completed their childbearing within the first five years, but found themselves still in the middle of it. They had become Postponers by default, part of the general trend towards postponement in their generation.

Home ownership had been achieved by fifteen out of nineteen Early Nester couples. They preferred to locate in suburban tracts of newly built homes with three or more bedrooms, two baths, two-car garages and state-of-the-art amenities, such as microwave ovens, trash compactors and green house windows. Although some had purchased older and smaller homes, it was clear that they wanted to trade up to a newer and larger model someday. Compared to Postponers, half of whom were still renting, the Early Nesters had rapidly put down roots in the first five years, seeing home ownership and parenthood as two sides of the same coin.

Although secure incomes had made it possible to buy a home in the early years of their marriage, it had also meant remaining on a plateau of education, occupation and income. After five years, most of the men were employed in the same blue collar or service jobs they had when they married. They had not pursued higher education. Neither had their wives, most of whom were only qualified for clerical, secretarial or retail sales jobs.

Jobs, homes and children were the exterior structure of their lives, but what of their sense of personal fulfillment? As they approached their thirties, they were generally optimistic about the future. Although moving a little slower than they had planned, they felt that they were on the road to fulfilling many of their dreams. The majority indicated that their marriages were "very satisfactory." Where each carried out their duties, marital conflict was usually a low-key affair. The husband still saw himself as the head of the household, but the power of the wife had increased substantially after the first child was born. The home and children were her domain; she made decisions about it, without much fear of contradiction. She raised the children as she saw fit, usually without much consistent help from him. He was deeply involved with earning a living, sometimes taking extra jobs, 'moonlighting,' to earn more money. Since they moved in different worlds of work and leisure, there were less occasions to argue. The remarks of one wife summed it up for most:

"We just want to live together with as few hassles as possible and be content with one another."

Beginning a family brought them a strong sense of accomplishment and completion:

"We are a family now, not just two people with a relationship."

". . . a marriage without children is incomplete. Our little girl has so enriched our lives that we wonder if we were really alive before we had her."

They spoke of newfound satisfactions:

"It's wonderful work, an unending joy."

"We had a child out of a sense of tradition, 'the thing to do', but now we find it very rewarding, caring for and instructing our child."

And they described the benefits it had brought to their marriage:

"We have become even closer now that our love has given us a beautiful son, wrote one mother. We just can't believe it! When I look at my husband, I see a new side of him I hadn't seen before. He is extremely gentle and playful with our baby. She added, I am proud of him for being such a very good father"

They had more at stake in keeping the marriage intact, as this husband explained:

"The child has been a positive factor, perhaps causing us to work harder on our marriage, where we might otherwise chalk it off."

The transition to parenthood was not without problems, however. Couples found themselves giving up some of their favorite pastimes, sacrificing the time that they had for themselves. The responsibility of raising a child resurrected some former problems and also added new ones, as this Early Nester husband relates:

"We argue more lately about paying our bills and about how to raise the child. It's been hard on our relationship because we thought we had these things settled."

For some couples, especially those who did not feel economically secure, the early months of parenthood were clearly a time of crisis.[13] The wives felt overburdened at times, continually occupied in a round of infant care interspersed with housework:

"Almost all of my time is spent with our two kids now, which leaves much less time for my husband. I'm afraid we are losing contact with each other."

The husbands, while proud to be new fathers, had feelings of being replaced as the focus of their wives' attention. They sometimes felt outside of the primeval circle of mother and infant:

"Naturally, more attention is directed away from me. . . ."

"Our sex life has faded. It's more like Mom and Pop Sex, now."

All considered, however, both husbands and wives appeared satisfied with their lives and optimistic about their future. They believed that their situations would improve as the husbands' income grew. They enjoyed their children and believed that parenthood would become less demanding over time. They looked forward to reclaiming their leisure when the children were older. Wherever the road might lead, they felt that the achievement of home ownership and parenthood, a new family unit, would not pale into insignificance. All else was secondary at this time.

EARLY NESTERS: AN OVERVIEW

The parents of Early Nesters had important characteristics in common. They were generally what sociologists would consider lower middle-class as measured by their educational and occupational status. On the average, they had a three or four children, cared for by a nonemployed mother. They were stable in residence and tightly connected to a network of relatives. Family bonds were idealized, although sometimes laden with unresolved conflicts and rivalries. Their marriages were rarely terminated by a divorce. Another important characteristic, we believe, was the strength of attachment with their married children. They called and visited frequently and helped in many ways, even with the purchase of a home.

Daughters were discouraged from activities that would take them out of the home. After high school, the daughters were not allowed to move out unless they married. Implicitly discouraged from preparing for a career, they were instead encouraged to make a youthful marriage. Finding their identity in relationships with others and lacking serious career interests, they devoted themselves single-mindedly to finding a potential husband. Getting married appeared to offer the most romantic escape from their home. The result was often a child-bride who concealed her pervasive dependencies behind a facade of girlish charm.

Sons, on the other hand, were expected to take steps towards a resourceful independence. It was hoped that they would get enough training to secure a well-paying job. Some emphasis was put on their future role as a family-provider but they were allowed "... to sow some wild oats, before settling down and supporting a family." In their search for potential wives, they pursued, and were pursued by, young virginal females. They wanted nurturing, home-oriented girls who would bring stability into their lives. Laying aside their dreams of youthful adventure for a steady paycheck, they took pride in their role as a provider.

The Early Nester marriage was like the two opposing blades of a scissors; it worked if each carried out their respective duties. Each was responsible for their own domain. He would help with the housework and the children but not consistently. She might work to help him meet the bills. Having little experience with the other's world they found it difficult to communicate across the chasm separating them. The husband spent a large share of his leisure time in a variety of masculine activities and the wife

73

became involved in a round of baby showers, home-demonstration parties, coffee klatches and television serials.

Whereas they had originally embraced these roles whole heartedly, some began to feel trapped in them as the years of marriage went by. They wondered if they had ". . . married too young," ". . . made the right choice" or ". . . had children too soon." Some women realized that if the marriage floundered, they would be facing a sharp reduction in income. For example, a recent study of women's employment has reported that: ". . . early childbearers have larger families, complete less schooling, obtain less work experience, consequently they earn less themselves, and other family members earn less. . . ."[14]

Although the majority of Early Nester marriages were apparently stable, we wonder what might be ahead for some. Limitations on travel, on leisure activities, on development of interests may be resented. The rapid foreclosure of educational and career opportunities may lead to nagging regrets and future recriminations. Some may wonder why they had children on the threshold of adulthood. These potential sources of discontent, aside, we think that most of our Early Nester couples will remain married although some unhappy marriages may be terminated, if the wife believes that she can support herself. In the next chapter, we will describe those who took an alternative path and waited five or more years before beginning a family.

Postponer Couples 6

THE NICHOLS: A POSTPONER COUPLE

Half of our newlyweds planned to wait five or more years before having a child. Eighty-two newlyweds wished to postpone parenthood. In this chapter, we follow their lives from childhood into the early years of their marriage. We'll begin by describing Jerry and Wendy Nichols, in many respects a typical Postponer couple.

It had been a long interview on that warm evening in May, and we were grateful for the cool breezes coming through the window of the second story apartment where the Nichols lived. Jerry and Wendy Nichols, married almost two years, were living in a one-bedroom apartment, furnished with an assortment of hand-me-downs. A large bird cage housing Wendy's "first pupil," a parakeet named "Mr. Pip", dominated one corner of the living room and added his voice to our tape recording of the interview.

Jerry Nichols, age twenty-five, was tall with an athletic appearance. He was in his last quarter at the university and working thirty hours a week as a delivery driver for a photo development company. His present job, he assured us, would not become his life's work. He was in the midst of sending applications to several universities where they had doctoral programs in Geography. His busy schedule began at dawn every day with a three-mile run over a hilly road. Jerry, the second of three sons, excelled in school, was the photographic editor of the high-school yearbook, and also ran for the track team. Both he and Wendy grew up in the same middle-class suburb, which was proudly shown to visiting city planners as a model of community planning.

Wendy, the oldest of two daughters, experienced the quarreling and eventual divorce of her parents while she was in elementary school. A few years later, her mother remarried and had two more children. Wendy did well in high school and was involved in several extra-curricular activities. Her mother, a former prom queen, encouraged her to enter the school's annual beauty pageant. Wendy recalls that she resented her mother's exhortations ". . . that I be the best in everything" and took to eating her school lunch alone to avoid ". . . the Status-Olympics." After graduating, Wendy worked for six months in a plant nursery and then spent her savings on a tour of European countries. After returning home she enrolled in the local community college.

Wendy, a very pretty, brown-haired, brown-eyed young woman, met Jerry on a geology field trip:

"I'd seen him in class and on the campus once in a while and he was very quiet, but very brilliant and was so curious that I would get butterflies in my stomach when I glanced at him."

They saw each other a great deal after that field trip; often spending time studying together. At the end of her freshman year, Wendy's family moved to a farm in Georgia and she reluctantly went with them. After six months, she returned to the Bay Area; enrolled in college and lived with her cousin. After a few months, she moved into Jerry's small studio apartment. His parents considered them to be ". . . living in sin" and strongly disapproved. Wendy's parents in Georgia suspected their cohabitation, but accepted it as a trial-engagement. Nevertheless, it was Wendy who suggested that they get married:

"One day I asked him 'Why don't we just get married on our quarter break?" He goes 'Why?' I told him that everyone would accept us; that it would be better. He felt it wouldn't really make much difference one way or another. So I go 'Well let's get married then."

They had a small wedding attended by their parents and a few friends. After a week's honeymoon, camping near Lake Tahoe, they returned to rent a one-bedroom apartment close to the State University. They both carried a full load of classes and worked part time. Towards the end of his undergraduate studies, Jerry was accepted in the doctoral program at a nearby university and promised a stipend for graduate study. They decided to pursue their studies, and postpone a family until they were each established in their respective careers. Three years later, we heard from them when they returned our follow-up questionnaire. They invited us to drive over and have dinner with them. Their apartment, even smaller in size than the one where we first interviewed them, was intensively utilized, enforcing an almost submariner's existence upon them. A used dishwasher and a new sofa bed were their only new furnishings. After a delicious dinner, which Wendy prepared in a ship's galley of a kitchen, they discussed their plans for the future. They planned to remain in their apartment until Jerry had written a dissertation and earned his doctorate in Geography. They hoped to buy their own house and start a family soon after he began teaching. Wendy would take a year's leave when a child was born and then resume her career. Until then, they felt they must make sacrifices. Wendy spoke about an abortion she had:

"I felt the loss of a potential. I had a special feeling when it was inside of me. I kept thinking it would be something that Jerry and I had created together. After I had the abortion, I felt down because it wasn't there anymore."

From all indications, they had become emotionally closer since we first interviewed them. Surrounded by couples in similar circumstances, they did not seem to mind the deferment of higher incomes. On the contrary, they were satisfied with the lives they were leading and radiated a sense of aliveness and interest in life. Wendy, especially, seemed more confident—no longer the "childwife" she had once called herself. As we said our farewells and walked to our car, Jerry called out: "See you on the talk shows. Remember, you're going to make us famous!"

POSTPONERS: A FAMILY PORTRAIT

Newlyweds, like Jerry and Wendy Nichols, who followed postponer timetables, usually came from families who were upwardly mobile. Many of their fathers had pursued higher education as a route to career mobility; nearly a third were college or university graduates. The majority held white collar positions in corporations or government offices and one in five had professional qualifications. Although a third of their mothers had been to a college or a university, the great majority were full time homemakers. There was a distinct tendency to have smaller families; two or three children were the norm. Social mobility undoubtably had a strong influence on the timing and number of their children.[1] Although more educated and upwardly mobile, it would be wrong to conclude that Postponers were mostly of white collar origins. In our sample of Postponers, for example, 32% of the wives and 43% of the husbands came from blue-collar backgrounds.

A substantial proportion of these families, 39%, had been destabilized by a divorce or a loss of a parent. It was also apparent that they were more residentially mobile. Many were recent arrivals in the Bay Area. All in all, they were less involved with their relatives and less traditional in their values than the parents of Early Nesters. In their recollections of family life, one theme stands in bold relief: Postponers were more detached from their parents than Early Nesters. They did not want to model themselves after their parents and were more critical of their shortcomings:

"Using my own parents as an example, I would say that the older generation was hung up on making it for making-its-sake. They rated people by their tract homes, their two or three cars, and other measures of affluence."

They were much less prone to see their parent's marriage as ideal. Approximately one out of three saw their parents as "not at all close" and the remainder were likely to describe them as only "moderately close". They spoke openly about their parent's problems, telling for example, of their father's heavy drinking or their mother's bouts of depression and flights into illness. Unlike Early Nesters, who typically described their parents in generalities, like: "normal," "average," "typical," "happy," and so on, Postponers gave a more balanced appraisal:

"They have frequent fights. My mother still has a persecution complex and she is a very difficult person to live with. But I wouldn't want to say that they had a bad marriage because they have been together for 27 or 28 years and I don't want to say they have a good marriage because they do fight all of the time. . . ."

In essence, Postponer women, were uninterested in becoming full-time housewives. They saw their mother's lack of fulfillment and were determined to avoid it:

"It has taken a lot of conscious effort on my part to try and not be like my mother. My mom is not an ambitious person. I feel sad about this and I think she does too, because she has never had enough motivation to do what she wants except to be a mother, and I feel like she isn't fulfilled totally."

Postponers appeared to take a more complicated, and longer route to discovering their values and goals. Whereas the Early Nesters had decided by late adolescence, essentially, who they were and where they were going; Postponers were more uncertain in their early twenties, remaining for several years in that stage of tentative commitments known as Youth.

Whereas the parents of Early Nesters controlled the lives of their daughters after they had graduated from high school; the parents of Postponers were tolerant of their children's outside involvements. This outward focus and openness to the larger society is captured by this wife's account of her mother's advice:

"Like my mom told me on my 18th birthday, 'You're raised. This is it! I'm not raising you anymore. You have been formally raised. . . . Consider yourself raised!' She expected me to 'live it up', because she lived it up in those years and she said, 'If you don't, you'll regret it, so go, have a good time, and try to find yourself in there some place. . . .' "

These upwardly mobile, middle-class families fostered their children's aspirations for a career. They were encouraged to follow their dreams wherever they might lead. "They journey of a thousand miles begins with one step," observed the sage Lao Tzu, and for Postponers that first step was to leave home.

LEAVING HOME: CAREER BOUND

"The process of separation proceeds along many lines. Its external aspects may involve moving out of the familial home, becoming financially less dependent, entering new roles and living arrangements in which one is more autonomous and responsible. Its internal aspects involve an increasing differentiation between self and parents, greater psychological distance from the family, and reduced emotional dependency on parental support and authority."[2]

As Levinson describes, leaving home proceeds at an emotional level, as well as in merely residential terms. The young man or woman must take up the challenge of separating themselves from their parents, as well as from their home. The majority of Postponers left home between their eighteenth and twentieth year, usually a few years because they were married. More than two-thirds claimed to leave for praise-worthy reasons, such as going away to college and to pursue career possibilities. But one in four said that the most compelling reason was to avoid conflicts with their family:

> *"The reason I moved out was for privacy. My folks always wanted to know where I was going and when I would be home. I thought I was old enough to do what I wanted to do."*

They were dissatisfied with the limited horizons of their family:

> *"It was a run-of-the-mill family; nothing to inspire any activities. Everything centered within the circle of the family: nothing exciting, nothing new, no imagination. We didn't take trips; we didn't go anywhere. We didn't do anything to inspire the imagination. It was very routine and eventually became dull and monotonous."*

Leaving the parental home became an almost sacred mission:

> *"I was going through that stage where you question everything, trying to establish your own direction. . . . It was like trying to break the umbilical cord."*

However, it might take a minicrisis to convince them it was time to move out:

> *"My mom felt that my hair was too long. She was worried that the neighbors would think I was on dope. She told me, 'Cut it or leave,' so I left!*

They resisted the temptations to settle for a local job:

> *"I was aware that I was getting older and that if I stayed at home I would become very dependent on the already existing strong family ties. I could see that I could easily get a job after high school with the company that my father worked for. You see, I didn't want to get involved in that; I wanted to lead a life of my own. I figured that if I could just break away and venture forth on my own I would be much more of a man than if I stayed at home. Things would be too easy for me at home."*

Traveling gave some an opportunity to take more responsibility for themselves:

> *"We bought ten speed bicycles and toured England and Scotland. We met people in the towns and they often put us up. Carol and I each brought only four hundred dollars and we couldn't go home and say, 'I'm hungry.' So we really had to make our money last."*

Living away from home allowed them to experiment with various lifestyles, as this woman's account of meeting her future husband suggests:

"We didn't say too much at first, but as the evening went on, we found that we had a lot in common and really got into some deep discussions. As time went on, we got more stoned, drank more wine, talked and laughed a lot, and somehow I ended up in the same sleeping bag as he did."

While Early Nesters carried out a struggle for emancipation while living at home, Postponers did so on a broader front. They did not simply press for fewer restrictions, but to live as adults. But the process of extricating themselves from their homes did not always proceed in a smooth fashion. They occasionally found themselves without money for rent and retreated home:

"I was a freshman when I decided to move out. At that time, I was making four hundred a month and I thought that would be plenty to share an apartment and live on. As it turned out, it wasn't. Finally, my father suggested that I move back home and save my money for a while."

These return trips were considered as temporary expedients. Having experienced a sense of independence, they found it harder to live under their parents' roof again, and made plans to move out as soon as possible.

Postponers usually had lived away from home for two or three years before they married. An apartment shared with same-sex roommates was their typical living situation. Although these arrangements sometimes led to disputes over "territorial rights" or "unmatched biorhythms" and so on, they provided valuable experience in living with peers and sharing household responsibilities. Another important advantage was that of having a wider field from which to choose potential mates. They dated more widely and generally had more love affairs than Early Nesters had. Also, courtships were of longer duration:

". . . in my junior year, we got engaged. We planned to get married before we did, but Uncle Sam interrupted those plans. So out of sheer desperation we waited until Bill came home and I graduated from college and then we got married. Since we started dating each other about three years before, we certainly didn't rush into marriage."

Almost half of the women and a third of the men lived with their future spouse before marrying them. They saw cohabitation as a way to test their compatibility as partners. Engagements frequently took the form of an understanding that they would marry whenever circumstances permitted. Since they were not living at home, their parents were less involved in arranging a large formal wedding:

"We got engaged at Christmas, moved into this apartment in February, and were married in August. There were no problems and her parents never hassled us. . . ."

80

Even when they did not experience pressures to 'make it legal,' they found their relationship became more acceptable when they married:

"After we got married, the next thing you know they were talking to me. They came out, bought us a bedroom set, bought us a kitchen set, they stayed with us, they filled the pantry, they filled the refrigerator, they did everything they could for us, because now it was acceptable in their eyes."

Postponer weddings were smaller. Over half had less than fifty guests. In essence, Postponer couples saw the wedding as a confirmation of their ongoing relationship. Marriage, in their eyes, had changed little except that they were now licensed to live together as husband and wife. Afterwards they returned to their jobs and studies, picking up the threads of their lives where they left them.

THE POSTPONER TIMETABLE

Postponer couples took a long-term perspective on their future married lives. They planned to devote the first five or more years to achieving a good marital relationship, to building careers, and creating enough credit to purchase their own residence. The pursuit of these goals fostered a sense of readiness to begin a family. In many cases, it would take several years to master these challenges, years during which most Early Nesters had already completed their childbearing.

The first task facing Postponers was to work out an egalitarian marriage. There was much more to be worked out, compared to Early Nesters where the husband was ostensibly the head of the house. Since they did not simply adopt traditional roles, they had to create their own, custom-made, division of household chores. Since most wives worked while their husbands finished their education; they were unable to assume sole responsibility for a smoothly running household. It was necessary for the husband to take care of daily chores no matter how inept or unwilling he was at first. Postponers were like two cross-country truck drivers who agreed on their destination, but not on the best route to get there. In the ensuing give-and-take, they laid the ground-work for an egalitarian relationship, a sharp departure from the more segregated roles played by their parents' generation.

An egalitarian partnership was not readily achieved. Each had to shed many of their former expectations about the proper roles of husband and wife. At times, a state of confusion prevailed about ". . . who should do what and how it should be done." They did not enjoy the Early Nester's sense of certainty. In contrast, more than half of the Postponers claimed: "There is no boss in this marriage." Shopping, cooking, laundry and housecleaning were done by both. Important decisions were based upon consensus. A marriage with equal rights and equal responsibilities was the cherished hope of these Postponers. Although they had not achieved equality, many seemed to be headed in that direction.

Postponers considered higher education as the royal road to an interesting, responsible and well-paying position: "I want a decent job where I can tell others what to do, instead of having everyone tell me what to do!" They were, without a doubt, quite serious about their career dreams. Earning a college or postgraduate degree was the immediate goal of Postponer women, we found. It was not a mere fantasy, the majority were determined to finish their studies. In addition to fulfilling their ambitions, it was seen as a source of security. One wife saw the situation faced by her generation in this way:

> "When my folks were first married, they only thought about raising a family, while we are concerned for ourselves right now and making good before having a family. There was always a job then and you could start a family easily, but now good jobs are not as easy to get and you want security before starting a family."

As we stated earlier, Postponers were slower to decide upon the goals they would follow. Career dreams rarely emerged fully fashioned, but developed in response to the possibilities that were taking shape. Their goals developed in stages which were not readily apparent even to them:

> "I went through the stage of depression where I didn't know what I wanted or anything. So I decided I'd better decided on something so that I'd feel better, and I did"!

Sometimes their spouses encouraged them:

> "He said, '. . . get your ass back to school, because you're not satisfied.' He could tell right away."

Of the forty-one Postponer husbands, only one saw raising a family as his clearest present goal. As a group, these men were career-oriented; the great majority were actively preparing for business or professional careers. Although both husband and wife were planning careers, the highest priority was given to launching the husband's. Finishing his education took precedence, with the understanding that: "You help me finish and then I can help you." It was expected that they would support each other rather than rely upon their parents' help. In light of these demands, it was understandable that they complained that completing their education was a long and tedious grind. They saw their time devoured by a constant commute between home, school and job. They saw themselves as "always rushed," "overwhelmed," and "already burnt out." Since they had to play several demanding roles without feeling quite competent, a sense of control seemed just beyond their grasp.

The final step to starting a family, in the minds of most Postponer couples, was to buy a home. Unlike their European counterparts, they rarely considered raising children in an apartment. On the contrary, they saw home ownership as an essential part of 'The

American Dream.' Encouraged by the media ". . . to enjoy the good life now" and trying to save for a down payment, they found themselves caught in a fiscal double-bind. Unless they had well-paying jobs and financial help from their families, their dream of buying a home seemed to recede into the distant future.

Raised during a time of widespread home ownership following World War II, baby-boom newlyweds assumed that they, too, would share in 'The American Dream' only to discover how difficult it had become. Robert Gunther, of the *Wall Street Journal* explains why:

> *"During the 1960s and early 1970s, the real income of U.S. families rose faster than housing costs, bringing home ownership within the reach of more people. Then from 1974 the trends were reversed. The median price of a new home jumped 81% through 1980; greater than the 68% rise in median family income. The gap widens even more when higher interest rates are figured."*[3]

> *"First-time buyers have been squeezed out, as a result. In 1977, 36% of those who bought homes were doing so for the first time. But by 1979, the percentage of first time buyers had shrunk to 18%."*[4]

A sudden awakening to the realities of the housing market aroused widespread concern in this generation of young marrieds:

> *"There was the lost generation after World War I, the beat generation of the 1950s, and the 'me' generation of the 1970s. Today, many young people talk of themselves as the "rent generation"—one that won't be able to afford a home."*[5]

A SENSE OF READINESS

> *"I'm not having a child unless I know within myself that I'm ready psychologically, jut the whole bit. I've got to be ready to devote myself to my children because I devote my time to my husband now."*

As this wife relates, Postponers, even those who were already established in a career, still did not think that they were emotionally ready to bring children into their lives yet. A good many were not willing to limit their career possibilities or leisure activities. Even after they had achieved the other prerequisites, there usually remained some personal considerations to be resolved.[6] Perhaps their most common concern was that they lacked the emotional resources to raise children according to their own, rather high, standards:

> *"If I'm in the mood and I see a baby, a cute little baby, I just get overwhelmed. But actually I'm not ready. For example, our little puppy, Alfie, he's just like a baby. I can't keep up with Alfie, let alone a baby."*

Some feared the intrusion of the child into their lives:

> *"I do want kids but not right now. I'm afraid that if I had some little toddler walking all over me, all the time, my feeling would be 'Leave me alone!'"*

Others wondered if their new-found sense of freedom might be eclipsed:

> *"A lot of people are involved with their own thing and don't have the time and patience to raise a kid. That's the way I feel right now. I'm just working my own head out. I'm afraid that I'd start feeling that the child was a burden, that it was bogging me down, I can't go anywhere because the kid's too little."*

Personhood before Parenthood was their unspoken motto:

> *"You see, if I don't fulfill my own goals and needs then I can't help my child. Therefore, the first priority is never to forget yourself because if you do that, you take advantage of your child. You are insecure and the child feels it."*

Postponer husbands wanted more time to get ready for parenthood. They were not so eager to become a father, as Leonard Benson writes:

> *". . . fatherhood, like marriage itself, is less important to men than motherhood is to women, in spite of the fact that maternity causes severe limitations on women's activities."* [7]

The fact that their husbands had lengthier timetables was a definite concern for some wives:

> *"If this were something I could do alone, it would probably be done by now. But it's a little hard. I'm not going to go out and just find someone I could have a baby with."*

As we listened to their views on fatherhood, one issue stood out and was related to many others; they were afraid of entrapment. They worried about being immobilized and trapped in many forms. The most common one was being stuck in an unrewarding job with little chance for advancement. Their emotional readiness for fatherhood seemed to rest mainly upon future career satisfactions. Since these concerns could readily be translated into financial ones, they often justified their reservations on those grounds:

> *"I tried to explain to her that you're responsible for that kid for a long time. Right now we couldn't afford it. I hope she sees my point. I hope she won't get bored and become one of those nagging housewives."*

Realizing that it would probably take longer than five years to achieve their financial goals, they justified postponement as an opportunity to enjoy life as a couple:

"I want Barbara and me to travel. That's what I really want. I just want to go out, to enjoy it before we get hung up on a bunch of little traps."

They looked upon this time of life as one of exploration and mobility, sometimes expressed in an interest in 'speed toys':

"If I were rich, I wouldn't own a lot of cars. I'd just have one. It's called the Jensen Interceptor II. They are beautiful cars. I would probably own an airplane or two. I'd go sailing in my own sloop. . . ."

Just as these couples hoped to reach their career and financial goals, they hoped that they would come to have a clear sense of readiness to have children. They admired a planned approach to life; expressed by this wife's summation of her goals in life:

"My goal is to feel that I've lived life to its fullest, especially as a woman. To do the right thing at the right time."

FIVE YEARS AFTER THE HONEYMOON

To a large extent, Postponer couples had achieved the career objectives they set themselves earlier. Follow-up information from twenty Postponers, fourteen wives and six husbands, fulfilled their own predictions. After five years of marriage, all but three had completed their degrees. Eight had gone on to postgraduate work. Two husbands were managers, one owned an import shop, one was a teacher, and one a salesman. Six of the fourteen wives were in professional careers such as teaching, nursing or social work, and one held a managerial position. Five were involved in secretarial, sales or service positions. Only two were full-time housewives. The common pattern, then, was for *both* husband and wife to pursue careers.

But, they were not moving towards home ownership as rapidly as the Early Nesters. Less than half had bought a home, eleven of the twenty couples still lived in rented apartments or houses. Many were waiting for their career to take shape before they bought a residence. In the meantime, they concentrated on laying a groundwork, as this wife explains:

"We now have several rooms of furniture all paid for. I have a very good job which I am happy with and we have built up an excellent credit rating."

Most saw themselves as happily married and indicated that they were very satisfied with their relationship. A few however, acknowledged continuing problems:

"During the time we considered separation, we went into marriage counseling. It was an excellent experience and I would recommend it highly. Even if there were no marital problems, the discovery of self and how you interact with your partner are worth exploring. Alex and I are closer today than when we were first married. Marriage is not so stagnant as many young people think."

Postponers were interested in keeping the marriage ". . . growing and healthy" in much the same way that Early Nesters were in the growth of their children:

"Most of the recent marriage advice books, judging from their content, are written for middle-class females who fear that they lack the skills needed to meet today's high demands for marital fulfillment."[8]

A heavy sense of responsibility for the well-being of the marriage rested upon the wife's shoulders and led her to try to transcend all limitations, to try to 'do it all', to be careerist as well as wife and mother. At times, the total demands required by all these endeavors could only be handled by the "Superwife" of television commercials. Most flesh and blood women felt overwhelmed as Marilyn Fabe and Norma Winkler describe in *"Up Against the Clock"*:

". . . as women take on demanding careers in addition to their responsibilities in the home, the danger emerges that the 'Mystique of the Feminine' so oppressive to our mother's generation will be replaced by the 'Mystique of the Liberated.' This new mystique embodies the notion that any woman should be able to manage both a career and a family; if anything goes amiss in either sphere, she has only herself to blame."[9]

Only three out of twenty Postponer couples had a child, none of the others were expecting one. Eighty-five percent were still childless after five years of marriage, a striking contrast to the Early Nester, where approximately the same proportion already had a child or were expecting one. Postponers were not only following their original timetable; they were lengthening it. The strong interest in having children had diminished considerably as this woman explained: "Children will not come into focus until I am ready to accept another role."

At this point, almost half of these couples were still undecided if they would have children at all. After a series of postponements, some might come to the decision not to have a child, as this husband foresees:

"The idea of not having children has crossed my mind, but I don't think I'll take that extreme either. I like children very much, but I don't feel ready to raise my own. I have discussed this feeling with Pamela many times and she seems willing to accept the delay. However, I'm not sure how she would react if I finally decided against children. This could cause some future conflicts or frustrations, but I hope we'll

work it out to our mutual benefit. We have always been able to compromise in the past, but child-rearing is a little tougher situation.''

A shift from postponement to voluntary childlessness would probably become a common occurrence for many middle class newlyweds:

"More childlessness results from decisions to delay births than from decisions against having children at all says Charles F. Westhoff, Director of Princeton University's Office of Population Research. Women are postponing childbirth until they are unable to have children or find themselves unwilling to give up a job or a lifestyle.'' [10]

In sum, it seems likely that a substantial proportion of postponers may decide after several years of marriage to remain childless. [11]

POSTPONERS: AN OVERVIEW

Postponement of parenthood is clearly on the rise among recently married American couples. The time interval between the wedding and the birth of the first child has lengthened substantially in the past decade. [12] And from all indications, it appears that postponed parenthood will become the norm as more married women continue working. [13]

Almost half of our newlyweds planned to defer parenthood. These individuals usually grew up in upwardly mobile, white-collar families where the fathers were college educated. A third, however, came from working class families, but these too were often upwardly mobile. Postponers were encouraged to do well in school and to become involved in school and community activities. Career aspirations were actively supported for both sons and daughters; they were expected to leave their families and make their way in the world.

The majority left home to attend a college or university before they were married. During these years, they lived away from home, and gained some experience in managing their own lives. They dated a greater number of people, and had more serious involvements. They usually took a longer time to marry than the Early Nesters. When they married, they had smaller weddings; especially if they had lived together before they married. They sought both an egalitarian marriage and satisfying careers. In addition, they wanted to become financially and emotionally ready to raise children. To achieve these objectives usually took longer than they had estimated. It was often necessary to lengthen their original timetable and postpone parenthood for a few more years. After five years of marriage, most Postponers had achieved their educational objectives and were beginning careers but still deferring parenthood.

Childfree Couples

THE PATTERSONS: A CHILDFREE COUPLE

The Pattersons, married a little over a year, lived in a high-rise apartment in Oakland. A large balcony complete with a cafe umbrella, table and chairs overlooked Lake Merritt and created a light and spacious atmosphere. Everything about their residence suggested a high standard of living for this dual-career couple. In describing their life, Pat Patterson emphasized the freedom it offered:

> *"Not having kids is a groove. We can come and go as we please. Sunday we might go down to Half Moon Bay and go horseback riding or body surfing. We might take a hike up Mount Tamalpais or tour the Wine Country."*

Pat, age 29, was the New Accounts Manager for a national moving van corporation and was also starting a trucking company of his own. A self-diagnosed 'Workaholic', he was proud of his accomplishments, and looked forward to becoming more successful in his field. Pat's father was an Air Force officer and his mother, a librarian. They gave Pat, their only child, material security, but in his eyes, not enough freedom. After his father died, Pat felt dominated by his mother, left home in Pennsylvania, and came to California.

Paula Patterson, age 26, a supervisor of patient services at a large hospital, was a slender young woman with reddish brown hair. Paula, the oldest of three children, grew up in an affluent suburb of San Francisco. Her description of her parents was rather jaundiced:

> *"My father is a businessman in every sense of the term. He doesn't show any empathy or understanding at all. I think that he is very cold toward people. He tries sometimes, but it is just beyond him. My mother is a 'ding bat'. She's gone! She verges on the role of neurotic and schizophrenic. I really don't know how to explain my mother. She is phony. She likes to be phony! She tries to be understanding, but she can only be nice to one person at a time. She could never love all three of us at one time."*

Paula refused to be married at the church where her parents worshipped, although they provided an elaborate reception:

"We had our reception at a country club with a band and a sit-down dinner. My mother, of course, went all out on the cake and catering, and on my dress. I don't think it looked any better than anyone else's though. . . ."

After their wedding, they lived in an apartment over one of her father's stores but soon moved to a downtown high rise ". . . in order to be closer to our jobs." Living farther away from her parents also kept their marriage more tranquil, they felt. Consequently, they only saw her parents on holidays and other special occasions; preferring to socialize with other couples.

Pat was resolved to become a successful businessman. He had procured several new accounts for his corporation and was confident that he could achieve as much with his own, still embryonic, company:

"I have already been fairly successful. I am well liked in the business. I have a good reputation. I am going in the right direction and I am going up."

Although he expressed a faint interest in having children after he was established, he seemed to be moving towards a decision to remain childless:

"I don't think that everyone is cut out to raise children. A lot of people have them because it's the thing to do. You know, keeping up with the Joneses, and that's a helluva excuse to have kids!"

While it appeared that Pat's interests in remaining Childfree expressed a wish for personal and career mobility; Paula's considerations had roots that extended into her unhappy childhood experiences:

"I have always been afraid of having children, that I would fail; that I would do something wrong and revert back to how I was when I was younger. I might be a little selfish in my attitude, but mostly I feel I'm being realistic. I spent twenty years not giving or sharing or receiving love. So how can I turn around and be loving and understanding to someone that is brand new?"

The Pattersons, contacted again in their fifth year of marriage, were living in the same high rise apartment building. Pat had resigned his position to manage his own company. In the interim, he had completed a Master's Degree in Business Administration. Paula had changed jobs and become a health educator. They had finally decided not to have any children:

"Overpopulation, world living conditions, poor schools, and the limitations it would put on our careers" was the tersely worded explanation that Pat gave. He added: *"I'm a rather selfish person and children would crowd my space."*

THE CHILDFREES: A FAMILY PORTRAIT

"Barren unions", "Childless Marriages", and "Nonparents" were the unflattering labels that have been used to designate married couples who haven't any children, whether by choice or because of infertility. Before the widespread availability of contraception, marriages without children were not common and considered unfortunate. Today, many cases of fertility impairment can be effectively treated, and it appears that the childless marriages of today are usually childless by choice.[1]

Voluntary childlessness shows clear signs of being on the increase in the industrial societies of North America and Western Europe. United States census data show that the proportion of childless women has ". . . increased from 24% in 1960 to 43% in 1977 for women 20 to 24 years old and from 13% to 24% for those 25 to 29 years old."[2] Apparently women in their twenties are postponing motherhood and a substantial proportion of them will remain childless. As we enter the last decade of this century, childless marriages will no longer be considered unusual, unconventional, or in some way deviant. Demographer Charles Westhoff predicts: "If current rates for first births were to persist, some 30% of U.S. women now of childbearing age would never have any children."[3]

As an example of this trend, a survey in Alameda County, California, where most of our sample of newlyweds reside, concluded that:

". . . young couples in the comparatively well-educated, disproportionately white collar population of Alameda County may have been a 'vanguard' in the movement to delay, limit or avoid parenthood that has since become more fashionable."[4]

There is a growing popular interest in childfree marriage. In the last decade, a number of books, such as Ellen Peck's *The Baby Trap* Anna and Arnold Silverman's *The Case Against Having Children,* and Elizabeth Whelan's *A Baby? . . . Maybe,* have appeared.[5] Although the current norm is a family with two children, a sizeable increase in one and zero-child families seems likely. If a significant proportion of Postponers decide after several years to remain childless, the number of Childfree marriages will increase. With these national trends in mind, let us look at the background of our Childfree newlyweds.

Seventeen women and seven men, 14% of our total sample, planned at the outset to have Childfree marriages. In contrast to the Postponers who wanted to wait for several years before starting a family, they had already decided that there never would be any children in their marriage. They were similar in many respects to the Postponers, coming by and large from more educated, higher income, and more mobile, smaller families. All were White except one Black and one Chinese woman. The majority were from Protestant backgrounds. They had the most education of our sample; and the women tended to marry a few years later than the other woman.

The fathers of Childfree newlyweds were the most highly educated ones in our sample, many had earned advanced degrees. They had careers as military officers, teachers, engineers, accountants, businessmen, hospital managers and journalists. They were described as hard working, upwardly mobile, strivers who often buried themselves in work. In contrast, their mothers were similar to the other mothers with respect to their modest level of education. Although several had been to college, few had stayed to finish a degree. Almost all were full-time housewives.

Although these families were similar to those of Postponers in most external features; a different impression emerges when we look more closely. Of all of the families, they had the greatest amount of emotional distance, tension and conflict between the parents. Over a third of these marriages ended in a divorce. Even when there hadn't been a legal rupture of the marriage, a state of emotional withdrawal and persistent conflict existed. In the opinion of two out of three childfree men and women, something was clearly amiss in their family. The home lives of many of these Childfree newlyweds left a good deal to desire:

"There was never any open affection shown in our house. My parents would never pick me up or kiss me like other parents do. I was kind of on the outside looking in."

The most scathing criticisms, and the most unflattering appraisals were leveled at their fathers: fourteen of twenty-four were very critical of him. Either he was completely absent, as in the cases of divorce or separation, or he was living at home, but was somehow unavailable, unapproachable, and in a sense, ". . . just not there!"; a complaint we were to hear frequently. A good many fathers were only peripherally involved in family concerns; their role was more or less limited to that of provider. This pattern which can be called "the absentee father" was composed of a husband who retreated from his wife and children into his work and hobbies, and a wife with few outside interests, who sought the meaning of her life in family roles. As he abdicated his position in the family, she moved in to replace him. To compensate for a host of unfulfilled expectations, she became overpossessive of the children, deepening the gulf between them and their father.

Demonstrations of affection between these unexpressive fathers and their children were rare:

"My father was very quiet. He was not at all affectionate; I can never remember sitting in his lap."

Even when he was physically present, he was still unavailable—barricaded behind a newspaper or a television screen, working alone in his study or in the garage:

"He was the one that I never saw and never talked to; he was just THERE!"

Eventually they came to resent his lack of interest in their lives:

"He always thought his damn business was more important. If any of us were in plays or even graduating, my dad never came to see us."

The absence of a close father-daughter bond can have a lasting effect on young women as psychoanalyst Marjorie Leonard found:

"When a father holds himself aloof, there is insufficient opportunity for day to day comparing and testing of the fantasied object with the real person. Moreover, consistent lack of attention is experienced as rejection which is destructive to the sense of self-esteem derived from the knowledge of being loved by an admired object."[6]

Four of the seven men also described their fathers as "distant," "withdrawn," or "uninvolved" or as excessively domineering and rigid. For example, one young man described his father, a high school coach, as a despot of the dinner table: "You could never reason with the guy because he always flies off the handle."

Not surprising was the tendency to limit conversation to the bare essentials necessary to live under the same roof, as Pat Patterson recalls:

"I just more or less ignored him. We didn't get along very well. I didn't think like he did and he could not, for the life of him, understand how I thought like I did!"

The mothers in these families often helped to exclude their husband from family matters. She used the barrier between the father and the children to better control each party, while appearing to protect them from one another. She played the role of power-broker by restricting the flow of communication between the children and her husband:

"He'd be the last one to hear of anything if something was to be said. I'd always communicate a problem to my mother first, and then we'd always try to keep it from my grandmother because she had a definite opinion on everything. Then we'd finally get around to telling my father."

As they grew older, some realized that their mother had capitalized on his lack of involvement. They came to resent her manipulative tactics, as this woman complained:

"I never really knew what my father's ideas were. If I wanted something, I would ask my mother, who would tell me that she would talk it over with my father. I never could get a hold of my dad to find out if that was really what he said. So I wonder how many times my mother lied to us about what my dad really felt."

While the father was a satellite revolving around the family's inner circle, the mother was most definitely its center. She had an enormous influence on her children and they developed an intense, but ambivalent, relationship with her. In their early years, they accepted her possessiveness but as they reached adulthood, many became wary of her efforts to control her family.

This family constellation, the distant father and the overcontrolling mother, has become enshrined in our national folklore. A good example is found in Chic Young's comic strip, 'Blondie,' whose husband, Dagwood, finds himself a visitor in his own home. As seen by Marshall McLuhan, Dagwood Bumstead's life, ". . . the diary of a nobody," reveals the eroding status of the middle-class American father:

"Blondie is trim, pert and resourceful. Dagwood is seedy, saggy, bewildered and weakly dependent. Blondie lives for her children, who are respectful toward her and contemptuous of Dagwood. Dagwood is 'living and partly living' in hope of a little quiet, a little privacy, and a wee bit of mothering affection from Blondie and his son Alexander. He is an apologetic intruder into a well-ordered dormitory."[7]

Although "the absentee father" was often roundly criticized by many Childfree newlyweds, it appears that the deck was stacked against him in some families. He was simply not a serious contender for the children's affection, in the opinion of attorney and psychologist, William Reynolds:

". . . she and the experts sadly agree that 'Yes, Father has indeed failed miserably here.' The kids haven't had a real father, you know, and it's only the mother's valiant, almost super-human efforts in the breach which have saved the kids from complete annihilation of the human spirit."[8]

In the same vein, sociologist Jean Veevers who studied childless wives in Canada states:

". . . many went on to report that their parents' marriage was a very unhappy one and that their mothers were basically unsatisfied with their housework and childcare roles."[9]

Undoubtably, many would-be-Childfree were reacting to the conflict ridden or stagnant relationship of their parents; although it is unlikely that all those who opted for a Childfree marriage had such emotionally impoverished home lives. These young people simply did not want to reenact their "family tragedy" by having children. In this regard, Andrew Hacker writes:

"Indeed about the worst thing that can be said of most people who have done well professionally is that they have failed as parents. Fear of such accusations may have caused many young people to be wary of starting families."[10]

In conclusion, our study indicates that newlyweds who chose a Childfree marriage at the outset typically experienced a family pattern where their fathers were fundamentally uninvolved while the mothers were often overinvolved in their children's lives.

Conflict and its avoidance seemed to permeate the daily lives of all family members. Given their dissatisfactions with their home life, it was not surprising that many were unwilling to begin a family of their own. One in three Childfrees did not, however, report such an unsatisfactory family life, but appeared to be attracted to the advantages of childlessness, rather than being repelled by parenthood, supporting the view of psychologist Edward Pohlman's that:

"When the culture has severe pressures against childlessness, a higher proportion of intentionally childless spouses are either somewhat maladjusted or strongly individualistic or both, although not all should be so classified. When pressures against childlessness are relaxed, a higher proportion of spouses choosing it are simply average people." [11]

THE FIRST TWO YEARS OF MARRIAGE

The first years of Childfree marriage were similar in many respects to those of Postponers'. They were also concerned with finishing their college education, beginning their careers, and dealing with household responsibilities. The crucial difference, however, between the Childfrees and the Postponers was a decision not to have children rather than deciding when to have them. In these years they were involved in building a "case against parenthood"—finding convincing reasons why they should remain childless. As time went on, they began to make a convincing case for a childfree marriage.

Childfree wives were the most educated in our sample, having more than three years of higher education on the average. Almost all were aiming at professional or business careers. They were apt to characterize housework as "fit for morons," or "slave labor". They preferred to spend their time on ". . . more rewarding activities" and resented expectations that they adopt ". . . a traditional role":

". . . sometimes there are indications that he wants me to play a traditional housewife role, like the old 'What's-for-dinner-tonight?' bit or the 'When-will-you-clean-up-the-apartment?' bit."

In spite of possible conflicts over role expectations, studies comparing the marital adjustment of childless couples report that they are not less adjusted or less happy than other married couples. Professor Angus Campbell, Director of the Survey Research Center of the University of Michigan, states:

"The decision not to have children does not doom a couple to loneliness, despair and misery as the prochildren forces have assumed for years. Childless husbands over thirty reported the highest satisfaction with life and they feel less pressure than most men." [12]

Childless wives also fared well. Professor Sharon Houseknecht of Ohio State University, who compared fifty voluntarily childless wives with fifty mothers, found that:

"The childless women expressed a stronger desire and determination to continue the marital relationship. They also reported a higher degree of happiness in their marital relationship relative to the happiness of most relationships than the mothers. . . ."[13] She concluded that: *"The results of the present study do not lend support to the notion that voluntarily childless women are more divorce prone than women with children."*[14]

Finally, Dr. Karen Renne, of the University of Arizona, analyzing the survey responses of 2,480 couples, came to the conclusion that:

"Childless marriages were more likely to be happy ones . . .; and the childless marriages tended to improve with time, while parents' marriages tended to deteriorate."[15]

Obviously, Childfree marriages can be both durable and satisfactory. To become so, they will probably come to a new perspective on childlessness, a process that we will now examine.

THE CASE AGAINST PARENTHOOD

"It seems like having kids is an unwritten law for being married and being a woman," said one disgruntled wife. Childfree newlyweds, like her, found themselves resenting pressure to have children at sometime in their married lives. They rejected the "cult of motherhood" and were determined to resist its devotees. Having children, they felt, should be a matter of choice rather than conformity to social expectations. They were contemptuous of those who jumped on the family bandwagon:

". . . at the moment, my generation considers it somehow fertile to have a child; the-renewing-the-earth-syndrome."

In their opinion, many young couples were taking the path of least resistance to please their parents or to hold their marriage together:

"As a child, I was socialized to believe that once a couple was married, the next order of business was to have a child."

Childfrees questioned the good sense of those who became parents because ". . . it was natural to have a child at a respectable and reasonable interval following marriage"; a common rationale for first pregnancies, according to Shirley Radl, author of

"Mother's Day is Over".[16] They saw television and the other mass media promoting "babysell," described here by Ellen Peck:

"Television has done a good job with some old messages: 'We've got a big country here,' say the Westerners; 'Motherhood is destiny' say the Soaps; 'Kids are fun for everyone,' imply the evening story lines; 'Life's real and high adventure is wiping up spills' say the advertisers."[17]

Whether by hard sell or soft sell they were told that motherhood was normal and childlessness was otherwise. Wilful refusal to have a child was indisputable evidence of a selfish, irresponsible and immature character. To counter these attacks on their self-esteem, they responded by sharply criticizing those who saw no alternatives to becoming housewives. One woman labeled them:

". . . your basic breeder. The wives are stupid; they have no common sense and can't do anything. All they want to do is watch soap operas. Many of them are fighting with their husbands all of the time and are in debt up to their ears. Yet, with a baby, they think everything will work out fine!"

A Childfree husband's appraisal was also unflattering:

". . . they all want to be housewives and live in big suburban houses in Orange County, surrounded by appliances and read only women's magazines and be as vacuous and superficial as they like!"

As they spoke of their aversions to becoming parents they dwelt upon the responsibilities they were loathe to assume:

". . . when you've got a child it's like you have this big, heavy suitcase full of bricks that you have to carry around that makes loud and unpleasant noises. Who needs it?"

Some felt that young children offered little in the way of companionship:

"I have nothing to say to a child. They're completely uninformed. You're better off talking to the plants or something. At least they don't say stupid things!"

When they weighed the value of having children, they wondered if the costs outweighed the benefits. In addition to financial costs, they were concerned about costs of a personal nature. According to psychologist Edward Pohlman:

"Parenthood costs in terms of mess, noise, confusion, general hubbub and strains and in terms of monotonous confinement for mothers. There is a decade of depression for many women between first pregnancy and the departure of the youngest child for school. Children may make it difficult for husbands and wives to find time

and energy for real communication and in other ways interfere with the marriage relationship.''[18]

Several newlyweds expressed fears that the arrival of a child would have a negative impact on their marriage. Children might come between them, they worried, create disagreements, and generally add new strains to their lives: ''More than anything,'' one man said, ''I want our marriage to be successful and a child might detract from that.'' His wife added, ''I feel that we don't need them. We can have a much better relationship without them.''

Whether children add or detract from a couple's relationship depends to a considerable degree on what they expect from their marriage. Children can make marital adjustment more difficult. Far from being a form of marriage glue, they may overtax emotional resources to the point where the couple withdraw from each other. For example, some wondered aloud if family responsibilities played a part in the impoverishment of their parent's relationshp:

''I guess I didn't really want to know why their marriage went wrong. I'd be afraid they'd say, 'We couldn't handle you kids'. . .''

A loss of physical attractiveness, as a result of having children, was of concern to some of the Childfree women:

''Many of the girls that I went to high school with that were beautiful have become fat and ugly, dumpy housewives!''

''I want to be able to enjoy the relationship with my husband and not have some teenager telling me that I'm fat, or that I have wrinkles—like I've seen a lot do.''

In the opinion of Ellen Peck, it is the wife who suffers most from childbearing:

''Children can turn a very nice girl into a frustrated nag. A rather beautiful friend of mine, for instance, has two children. She also has ulcers, colitis, hypertension headaches, a husband who avoids her and a hatred of existence in general.''[19]

And, she warns against turning one's home into a wall-to-wall nursery:

''You know, I think I could explain some divorces rather simply. Dad may simply have gotten fed up with all those Dresdenite-finished shoes, mini-vaporizers, cradalettes, musical floaters, Busy Boxes and little doodits and decided he wanted a dark beamed oak den, black leather sofa, fake zebra throw, a bar and a woman.''[20]

Parenthood can adversely affect a couple's sexual relationship, cautions writer Betty Rollin:

"Often when the stork flies in, sexuality flies out. Both in the emotional minds of some women and in the minds of their husbands, when a woman becomes a mother, she stops being a woman. It's not only that motherhood may destroy her physical attractiveness, but its madonna complex may destroy her feelings of sexuality."[21]

Where the marital relationship has been virtually submerged by the parental one, they might simply become partners in a 'Mom-and-Pop enterprise':

"She becomes so much the mother that she may one day find herself treating that tweedy, commuting chap who was once her husband and lover as just another one of the brood—another running nose to wipe, another mouth to pop a vitamin pill into, another finicky appetite to cater to, an over-grown petulant child. He even calls her 'Mom'. She calls him 'Dad' and that sums up their relationship."[22]

THE CASE FOR A CHILD-FREE MARRIAGE

As they peered down the road to their future, Childfree couples saw dimly at first, but then with more clarity, that childlessness offered them another path to fulfillment. They came to see their choice not simply as a negation of parenthood, but as a positive path to follow. Their self-image changed from childless to childfree. They saw their lives as career-focused, geographically mobile, and affluent. Not having a family meant an uninterrupted career for the woman, a higher combined income and far more leisure time. Compared to Early Nester and Postponer women, Childfree wives would be able to continue a full-time involvement with their careers. Many appeared to be headed towards professional careers: medicine, dentistry, audiology, nursing, microbiology, teaching and social work were some of the careers they sought. A smaller number aimed at careers in business. But a few worked as waitresses or clerks and were undecided about their future.

In addition to anticipated career satisfactions, they were attracted to the higher standard of living they would enjoy. For example, marriage researchers, Nason and Paloma found that:

"The advantages of joint incomes were mentioned time and time again by the couples and this monetary advantage seemed to play an important role in remaining childless."[23]

The career image of Childfree wives comprised an affluent lifestyle and the symbolic accoutrements of success: titles, private offices, expense accounts, etc. "Career-Chic," as one wife called it:

"What the magazines are going in for is no longer the married woman or the mother, but the Superwoman with the career, 'the Ms. Independent.' Like Glamour magazine, they used to show women on dates in beautiful dresses, and now they have whole sections on how to dress for success and that sort of thing."

The Childfree lifestyle conjured up vistas of a world of leisure possibilities unconstrained by family responsibilities; of visions of jet-set travel, Club-Med vacations to tropical shores, and weekends at mountain ski resorts. After work and on weekends, the Childfree couple could go to restaurants, concerts, art exhibits and a round of social events. On their vacations they could travel wherever their interests beckoned. When they were first married and finishing their education, these visions might be only fantasies; however, after they had careers, possibilities could become realities. Although they may not exercise all their options, they had the freedom to do so, and that became the essence of their lifestyle. They not only had "freedom from" family responsibilities; but they were gaining "freedom to" experience their version of the good life, a life of self-fulfillment as Professor Jean E. Veevers sees it:

> *"The child-free lifestyle is exclusively adult centered, in contrast to the child-centered worlds in which most lower and middle-class couples spend most of their middle years. The stress is upon adult entertainment and adult pleasures and recreations. Considerable emphasis is placed upon the intrinsic value of self-expression (such as painting or writing) and on self-improvement (such as continued education)."*[24]

To expand the dimensions of their world was of foremost importance to them:

> *"I want to be mobile, to get up and go when the spirit strikes me."*

> *"I wouldn't want them to tie me down. I want to pursue my career and do a lot of things I couldn't otherwise do."*

> *"The 'now thinking' is to avoid having children. We want to be free to do as we feel, to come and go as we see fit."*

and finally,

> *"If you want to climb to the top, then there is no time for children."*

Many of their statements reveal a strong preference for control over their own time. Time was considered a more precious resource than money:

> *"The main thing that appeals to me about not having children is time; time to invest in doing what I want to do on my own—growing."*

They did not relish the thought of waiting for the children to grow up and leave home, as this husband states:

> *"The only time I could see having one is if we both wanted to sacrifice the time, fifteen or more years of our lives just to get a human being off to the right start."*

Thus, their sense of freedom, so central to a child-free lifestyle, depended upon the illusion of the unconstrained use of leisure time. And their visions of leisure definitely did not include a round of P.T.A. meetings, Scout jamborees, Sundays in the park, or annual visits to Disneyland.

The Childfree were exploring a frontier of new possibilities. There were no well trod paths laid out in front of them. They had to choose their direction as they moved forward. Their vistas of freedom were at once exhilarating and disquieting, a sort of existential free-fall. If they were disenchanted with their neighborhood, they could move; if they didn't like their jobs, they could find others; and if they were seriously unhappy in their marriage, they could divorce. Since none of these changes would affect the welfare of children, there were few credible excuses for making the best of a bad situation. To be childless or to be childfree were, indeed, two sides of the same coin.

CHILDFREES: AN OVERVIEW

A good many childfree men and women in our sample of newlyweds had a very problematic family life. Their parents were emotionally divorced even if legally married. Not only were the parents alienated from each other, but often from their children, as well. The fathers were typically inexpressive and unavailable satellites revolving around the center of family life. In contrast, the mothers had few interests outside of the home. In spite of an intense focus on "her" family, she did not gain fulfillment from it. Many told of a prolonged struggle to free themselves of her "smother-love". Very few wanted a family life like the one they had experienced, an orientation which, we think, underlies the disinclination to have a family of their own.

During their courtship, the question of children was discussed, but was often left unsettled. They often did not fully disclose their reservations about having a child, for fear of weakening the relationship at its outset. Thus the final decision to remain childless usually came after a period of extended consideration. Although the inclination towards a Childfree lifestyle was formed earlier, it would usually take a few years before they both felt comfortable with their choice. The achievement of interesting careers, substantial incomes and a sense of personal freedom tipped the scale towards a childless marriage. They began to see themselves as a Childfree couple, rather than accept a stigmatized image as a Childless one. With more certainty about who they were and where they were going, they became more confident about showing themselves in a new light.

Becoming a Childfree couple involved building a convincing case against parenthood as a counterweight to traditional expectations. Parenthood was seen as an unrewarding, time-consuming, costly sacrifice which would entail a major interruption of the woman's career, a sharp drop in income and a substantial increase in living expenses. On the other hand, a Childfree marriage extolled the quest for self-fulfillment and a life rich in experience. The final decision to actively choose a Childfree life was made after weighing the arguments in the tribunal of their minds. In many respects, the process was similar to that undergone by Postponer couples, except that they came to the decision that ". . . there never was going to be a right time."[25]

A Travel Guide for Newlyweds **8**

THE NEWLYWED JOURNEY

The first year of marriage was essentially a continuation of a romance which began during their courtship. During this time, they were trying to adjust to each other, sharing their lives more completely than was previously possible. Of central importance was their willingness to communicate with each other. To build an authentic and intimate relationship, they had to risk disclosing the resentments and disappointments which inevitably surfaced. They learned to accept the childish and the adult, the angry and the loving; in a word, the dark, as well as the light, side of the other. Without an effort to reveal their differences, the relationship was in danger of losing its vitality. If they retreated from this challenge, they found themselves limited to a more constricted range of topics which were safe to discuss. Related to this effort at self-revelation was that of discussing their sexual wishes. The quality of their lovemaking, rather than its sheer frequency, would become a measure of sexual fulfillment.

Much depended upon their capacity to subordinate individual wishes to the best interests of the marriage; a capacity which rested upon a relatively secure sense of personal identity. First-year couples were extending their sense of "we-ness." They had the opportunity to convert a romance based upon projected fantasies into a partnership based on more realistic expectations. This monumental undertaking was not without casualties: those who recoiled from the initial disillusionment; those unwilling to risk a merger of destinies; and, those who preferred to live emotionally separate lives although sharing the same bed and board. Even those who mastered the challenge of intimacy found themselves facing a time of difficulties around the first anniversary, usually from the tenth to the fourteenth month of married life.

The romantic stage had run its course leading to a time of tension and doubts. At the outset, it was difficult for many couples to express their differences for fear of alienating the other and confronting their own angry feelings and disappointments. Instead, they preferred to wait until the relationship seemed more stable. They tried to preserve the illusion of harmony, hoping that their problems would fade away with the passage of time. However, this strategy of avoidance rarely worked and pent-up resentments surfaced with explosive force.

For many reasons, a time of conflict intervened between the Romantic and the Future-Oriented stages. This problematic interlude helped move the couple towards a more honest, less superficial, interaction. For this reason, we have come to regard this brief phase as the foundation of a healthier union. Contrary to the popular view that a happy marriage is one without disagreeable episodes, we have come to believe that such pseudotranquility may be a sign of personal and marital stagnation. Conflict, we found, if handled constructively, led to a clearer sense of direction, a deeper and more alive relationship. As psychoanalyst Eric W. Fromm writes:

> ". . . the conflicts of most people are actually attempts to avoid real conflicts. They are disagreements on minor or superficial matters which by their nature do not lend themselves to clarification or solution. Real conflicts between two people, those which do not serve to cover up or to project, but which are experienced on the deep level of reality to which they belong are not destructive. They lead to clarification, they produce a catharsis from which both persons emerge with more knowledge and more strength."[1]

Having weathered a brief session of storms, having tested their bond and strengthened it, the couple were ready to face serious questions about their future. The stage of Future-Orientation usually began well into the second year. It was characterized by a more realistic appraisal of the possibilities, the strengths and the weaknesses of their relationship. Above all, it was marked by a focus on the future. During this time the husband and wife tried to convert their dreams into a hierarchy of goals. They realized that if they were to achieve some of these goals they must begin to allocate their resources of time, money and effort. The resultant plan became their **Marital Timetable**. Once constructed, marital timetables took on a life of their own becoming a schedule for the couple to follow, a chronological yardstick by which they measured their progress.

Of singular importance, in our opinion, was their commitment to the timetable they had chosen. It became a road map for their journey, a master plan for realizing their dreams. In this respect, timetables were their grand strategy for playing the game of life. Given that their resources of time and money were limited, they had to decide which goals were most important and readily attainable. The specification of goals, their arrangement in terms of priority, the deployment of resources, and the scheduling of efforts were the common elements of all timetables. The basic issue which led to different marital timetables, however, was when to have the first child.

In our sample, 34% of the husbands and 42% of the wives chose an **Early Nester** timetable. They chose to have children early in adulthood and early in the marriage. They saw few compelling reasons to defer parenthood. They rapidly adopted the traditional marital roles of bread-winner and housewife. Wives did not continue in college but remained working until they had a child. Husbands sought secure, well-paying jobs rather than pursue distant career prospects. Contraception was relaxed as they used less reliable forms of birth control. The results were predictable; after five years almost all of the Early Nesters in our follow-up survey had a child. However, for a variety of reasons the next child was often deferred. They would not match their parents' reproductive efforts, efforts which had produced the demographic phenomenon known as 'the Baby Boom'.

Postponement of a family until the husband's and the wife's careers are launched seems to be shaping up as the norm for the present generation of young, middle-class couples. Approximately half of our sample, 58% of the husbands and 43% of the wives, had decided on this option. In the early years of marriage, they focused on laying the foundations for a dual-career marriage. They took time to decide if-and-when to have children. However, it appeared to be taking longer than the allotted five years for them to begin a family. They, too, had stretched their timetables.

The **Childfree** timetable was the least popular of the three; only 8% of the husbands and 15% of the wives chose it. Later, they would be joined by converts from the ranks of the Postponers. This timetable had a strong appeal to those women who were concerned that their freedom and their career opportunities would be sharply limited by the responsibilities of a family. In these years, Childfree couples would struggle with a difficult choice as they tried to separate their personal considerations from those of their families and friends. Since a considerable number of them had grown up in conflict-ridden families, they often saw parenthood as a form of martyrdom. As their careers developed, and other rewards began to accrue, they came to regard themselves as "childfree" rather than "childless." Their marital timetable became one whose milestones were degrees, promotions, and other symbols of personal achievement. While the rationale of the Postponer timetable was to prepare for careers and eventual parenthood, that of the Childfree was to invest in personal freedom and career mobility.

THE ROAD TO NOWHERE

Which of our newlywed marriages will survive and flourish and which ones seem to be headed for an early divorce? This question, in one form or another, comes up in any discussion of the newlywed years. Although statistical predictions can be made with some confidence, individual cases are inherently more difficult to predict. Nevertheless, it is useful to contrast two types of married relationships that we found in our study of young newlyweds. For the sake of simplicity, we will refer to them as *Evolving Relationships and Stagnating Relationships*. The latter tend to deteriorate to the stage where divorce is often seen as the best solution.[2]

In an **Evolving Relationship** the couple were able to move from present to future concerns, giving direction to their marriage by discovering their goals and creating a workable timetable to attain them. They were also able to keep a sense of emotional intimacy alive. They retained a romantic core to their marital bond and enjoyed spending time together. In essence, they were able to merge their destinies without submerging their identities.

In contrast, the most striking feature of a **Stagnating Relationship** was a communication blockage; a tacit agreement to avoid discussing certain important issues. As a result they lacked a sense of shared destiny. They were often unable to mobilize their resources to handle the serious problems which came their way. Usually, both experienced a profound sense of disappointment; their original expectations about marriage were not met and they could not accept the reality they found. Resentments were stock-piled, and each sought an escape from intimacy in separate leisure pursuits or perhaps through alcohol, shopping binges, extra-marital affairs and a variety of other temporary palliatives.

Whereas the majority of our newlywed marriages appeared to be moving forward, about 10 to 15% of the couples already showed unmistakable signs of early marital distress. We believe they were unable to make an acceptable transition from a romance to a married partnership largely because they could not agree upon a shared future. We think it is accurate, therefore, to designate these marriages as "stagnate", a condition which is the result of the loss of forward motion.

SEVEN POTENTIAL PITFALLS

Finally, we would like to offer some suggestions which we think are warranted in the light of our findings. We risk the hazards of offering advice in the hope that newly-weds can avoid some of these potential pitfalls.

HYPER-ROMANTIC COURTSHIPS

In our opinion, the American way of courtship suffers from an excessive preoccupation with glamorous dates, orchestrated engagements and fairy-tale weddings. As a creative alternative, couples could avail themselves of a wider range of activities and situations than is found in the usual evening dates. Camping, traveling, studying and working together, for example, offer excellent opportunities to know each other better. Where the couple's lack of readiness, or other barriers do not preclude it, cohabitation can also provide a realistic courtship. Although not without risks, it can offer the couple the chance to experience a marriage-like situation, to determine if they are compatible and reduce the likelihood of a matrimonial misalliance.

ESCAPE-HATCH MARRIAGES

Young adults recently out of high school, occupationally unskilled, and still living at home, stand on the very threshold of adulthood. They tend to see getting married as an escape from their now confining homelife, as a nonstop elevator to full-fledged adulthood. A considerable proportion marry before they are sufficiently detached from their parents. Given the high risk of divorce among these very young couples, it seems reasonable to postpone marriage until one has lived away from home for a while.

MEGA-WEDDINGS

Our study has led us to wonder if large, expensive weddings and catered receptions, contribute much towards a couple's future adjustment. On the contrary, we think they can detract attention from more serious issues. We'd suggest that the engaged couple give thought to scaling down their wedding preparations to less extravagant proportions. With less money and effort spent in arranging a large wedding reception, they might channel these resources into setting up a household, completing a degree or for other important purposes.

UNDERDEVELOPED TIMETABLES

Single people frequently regard the state of marriage as a final destination, a sort of happy-ever-after land. But it can be seen as a journey requiring directions and timetables. Timetables which were most effective were those which, although committed to certain goals, were nonetheless flexible in their pursuit of them. Above all, "these timetables" had to be capable of being elongated to handle unforeseen delays; destination was of more importance than the time it took to get there. Effective timetables provided several benefits to the couple: they reduced fruitless conflict, they increased the desire to communicate, and made for a stronger commitment to a partnership of shared work and shared rewards.

PREMATURE PARENTHOOD

In our study of newlyweds, we have found that the first two years of marriage were a time of profound adjustments for most couples. If the couple begins a family in the midst of these developments, they add heavy new responsibilities and additional problems to their marriage at a time when it is rapidly evolving and possibly quite fragile. We think that the present trend towards postponement of parenthood has much to recommend it. It allows the parties to develop patience, self-esteem, mature nurturance and other qualities thought to characterize good parenting.

ABORTED CAREERS

Some traditionally-minded young women give little thought to preparing for a fulfilling occupation. Since considerable financial resources are required to buy a home and provide for children, it no longer seems desirable to rely solely upon the husband's income. In addition to the desired standard of living, which a career offers, the personal satisfactions and sense of adult identity it provides are also of enduring value.

TOXIC CONFLICTS

Finally, it seems ironic that a society which encourages marriage and parenthood at a relatively young age, should express such dismay at the high divorce rate of these unions. Given the intense demands marriage can make, we should be surprised that so many survive and even flourish. Those who do so, we think, have learned to manage their conflicts in a constructive way. Rather than allow conflict to reach toxic levels, they use it to strengthen their relationship. If it becomes necessary to sever the relationship to save the parties, it is done in a way that minimizes the toxic residuals of a bitter divorce and allows them to go forward in their lives.

In the last analysis, perhaps the best advice one can give a traveler is to offer them as accurate and as detailed a road map as possible. We have tried to reconstruct the journey traveled by our newlyweds in the belief that rewarding marriages are based upon a clear notion of their destinations and the possible roads to them.

Notes

Foreward

1. Robin Worthington, "Dispelling the Myth of the Superwoman," *The Hayward Daily Review,* April 21, 1983.
2. Bureau of the Census, Current Population Reports, Series P-20 No. 297, *Number, Timing and Duration of Marriages and Divorces in the United States, June 1975,* U.S. Government Printing Office, Washington, D.C. 1976.
3. Some sections of the Newlywed Interview schedule were adapted from that used in the U.C.S.F. Adult Transitions Research Project where the author was a postdoctoral fellow. For a description of their interview schedule, see: Marjorie Fiske Lowenthal et al., *Four Stages of Life,* San Francisco, Jossey-Bass, 1975, pp. 247–249.

Chapter One

1. Edward Westermarck, *Marriage,* New York, Jonathan Cape and Harrison Smith, 1930, p. 1.
2. Pierre L. van den Berghe, *Human Family Systems: An Evolutionary View,* New York, Elsevier, 1979, p. 114.
3. Edward Westermarck, *A Short History of Marriage,* New York, MacMillan, 1926, p. 255.
4. Margaret Baker, *Wedding Customs and Folklore,* Totowa, New Jersey, Rowman and Littlefield, 1977, p. 45.
5. Marcia Seligson, *The Eternal Bliss Machine: America's Way of Wedding,* New York, William Morrow & Co., Inc. 1973, p. 36.
6. Diana Leonard, *Sex and Generation: A Study of Courtship and Weddings,* London, Tavistock, 1980, p. 123.
7. Diana Bright, *The Wedding Planner,* Los Angeles, Nash Publishing, 1970, p. 64.
8. Bright, ibid., p. 46.
9. Leonard, op. cit., p. 130.
10. Khoren Arisian, *The New Wedding,* New York, Vintage, 1973, p. 120.
11. Philip Wylie, *Generation of Vipers,* New York, Pocket Books, 1959, pp. 187–188.
12. Seligson, op. cit., p. 67.
13. *Better Homes and Garden's Bride's Book,* Des Moines, Publishing Group of Meredith Corp., 1982.
14. Jan Trost, *Unmarried Cohabitation,* Vasteras, Sweden, International Library, 1979, p. 25.

15. Ethel L. Urlin, *A Short History of Marriage,* Detroit, Singing Tree Press, 1969, pp. 181–182.
16. Baker, op. cit., p. 22.
17. L. F. Herze and J. W. Hudson, "Personal and Family Characteristics of Cohabiting and Non-Cohabiting College Students," *Journal of Marriage and the Family,* 1974, vol. 36, p. 726.
18. Charles F. Westhoff, "Marriage and Fertility in the Developed Countries," *Scientific American,* 1979, vol. 239, p. 54.
19. Seligson, op. cit., pp. 278–279.
20. Arisian, op. cit., p. 15.
21. Arisian, ibid., p. 89.
22. Bright, op. cit., dust jacket.
23. Leonard, op. cit., p. 267.
24. Basil J. Sherlock and Ingrid Moller, "Making It Legal: A Comparison of Previously Cohabiting and Engaged Couples," *Journal of Sociology and Social Welfare,* 1981, vol. 7, pp. 97–110.

Chapter Two

1. Diana Leonard, *Sex and Generation: A Study of Courtship and Weddings,* London, Tavistock, 1980, p. 235.
2. Arnold Van Gennep, *The Rites of Passage,* Chicago, The University of Chicago Press, 1960.
3. Elaine Walster and G. William Walster, *A New Look at Love,* Reading, Mass., Addison-Wesley, 1978.
4. Murray S. Davis, *Intimate Relations,* New York, The Free Press, 1973, p. 200.
5. Lillian Breslow-Rubin, *Worlds of Pain,* New York, Basic Books 1976, p. 149.
6. Eric Berne, *Sex and Human Loving,* New York, Simon and Schuster, 1970, p. 264.
7. Daniel Goldstine, Katherine Larner, Shirley Zuckerman, and Hilary Goldstine, *The Dance-Away Lover,* New York, Ballentine, 1977.
8. John F. Cuber and Peggy Harroff, *Sex and the Significant Americans,* Baltimore, Penguin Books, 1966, pp. 174–175.
9. Ann Oakley, *The Sociology of Housework,* New York, Pantheon Books, 1974, p. 141.
10. Marjorie Fiske Lowenthal, Majda Thurnher, and David Chiriboga, *Four Stages of Life,* San Francisco, Jossey-Bass, 1975, p. 69.
11. Ralph La Rossa, *Conflict and Power in Marriage: Expecting the First Child,* Beverly Hills, Sage, 1977, p. 151.
12. Jessie Bernard, "The Adjustments of Married Mates" in H. T. Christensen (editor), *The Handbook of Marriage and the Family,* Chicago, Rand McNally, 1964, pp. 675–740.
13. Angus Campbell, "The American Way of Mating: Marriage Si: Children, Only Maybe," *Psychology Today,* May 1975, p. 38.

14. Keith Melville, *Marriage and Family Today,* New York, Random House, 1980, p. 308.

Chapter Three

1. Daniel Goldstein *et. al.* "The Three Stages of Marriage," *Family Circle,* May, 1977.
2. Roger Gould, *Transformations: Growth and Change in Adult Life,* New York, Simon & Schuster, 1978, p. 121.
3. John F. Cuber and Peggy B. Harroff, *Sex and the Significant Americans,* Baltimore, Penguin Books, 1968, p. 49.
4. Daniel J. Levinson with Charlotte N. Darrow, Edward B. Klein, Maria H. Levinson and Braxton McKee, *The Seasons of a Man's Life,* New York, Ballentine Books, 1978, p. 91.
5. Levinson, op. cit., p. 97.
6. Levinson, op. cit., p. 109.
7. Warren Farrell, *The Liberated Man,* New York, Bantam Books, 1974, p. 85.
8. Levinson, op. cit., pp. 57–58.
9. Marjorie Fiske Lowenthal, Majda Thurnher, and David Chiriboga, *Four Stages of Life,* San Francisco, Jossey-Bass, 1975, p. 179.
10. Kristin Luker, *Taking Chances: Abortion and the Decision not to Contracept,* Berkeley, University of California Press, 1975, p. 65.
11. Julius Roth, *Timetables: Structuring the Passage of Time in Hospital Treatment and Other Careers,* New York, Bobbs-Merrill, 1963, p. 115.
12. Michael P. Fogarty, Rhona Rapoport, and Robert N. Rapoport, *Sex, Career and Family,* London, George Allen & Unwin Ltd., 1971, pp. 334–335.

Chapter Four

1. Weitzmann, Lenore J. *The Divorce Revolution: The Unexpected Social and Economic Consequences for Woman and Children in America,* 1985, New York, The Free Press. p. 15.
2. Weitzmann, op. cit. p. XVIII
3. Cherlin, Andrew. *Marriage, Divorce, Remarriage,* 1981, Cambridge, Harvard Univ. Press.
4. Mahmoundian, Showleh. *Marital Conflict of Newlyweds at the Preparental Stage of the Life Cycle.* 1980, Cal. State University, Hayward thesis.
5. Alvarez, A. *Life After Marriage: Love in an Age of Divorce.* 1981 New York. Simon & Schuster. p. 27–28.
6. Blumstein, Phillip and Schwartz, Pepper. *American Couples: Money, Work, Sex,* 1983, New York, Simon and Schuster. p. 201.
7. Blumstein and Schwartz op. cit., p. 312.
8. Blumstein & Schwartz op. cit., p. 313.
9. Blumstein & Schwartz op. cit., p. 110 & p. 313.

10. Vaughn, Dianne. *Uncoupling: Turning Points in Intimate Relations,* 1986, New York, Oxford Univ. Press. pp. 5–6.

11. Lederer, Philip and Jackson, Don. *The Mirages of Marriage,* 1968, New York, W. W. Norton p. 258.

12. Lederer and Jackson, op. cit., p. 119.

13. Mahmoundian, op. cit., p. 33.

14. Dicks, Henry V., "Experiences with Marital Tensions seen in the Psychological Clinic" in J. J. Howells (editor) *Theory and Practice of Family Psychiatry,* 1971 New York, Brunner/Mazel p. 274.

Chapter Five

1. Phillipe Aries, *Centuries of Childhood: A Social History of Family Life,* New York, Vintage Books, 1962, p. 406.

2. Lee Rainwater, *And the Poor Get Children,* Chicago, Quadrangle Books, 1960, p. 72.

3. Nancy Chodorow, "Oedipal Asymmetries and Heterosexual Knots," *Social Problems,* 1976, Vol. 23, p. 462. Also see: Nancy Chodorow, *The Reproduction of Mothering: Psychoanalysis and the Sociology of Gender,* Berkeley, University of California Press, 1978.

4. Diana Leonard, *Sex and Generation: A Study of Courtship and Weddings,* London, Tavistock, 1980, p. 214.

5. Wells Goodrich, R. G. Ryder and H. L. Rausch, "Patterns of Newlywed Marriage." *Journal of Marriage and the Family,* 1968, Vol. 30, p. 388.

6. Daniel Beaver, *The Marriage Fantasy,* Walnut Creek, California, Awareness Press, 1982, p. 29.

7. Beaver, op. cit., p. 31.

8. Jessie Bernard, *The Future of Motherhood,* New York, Penguin Books, 1974, pp. 21–22.

9. Michael Young and Peter Wilmot, *The Symmetrical Family,* Hammondsworth, Penguin Books, 1973, p. 91.

10. Patricia Walker Fine, "The Pro-Parental Path of Marital Transition," a paper presented to the Graduate Seminar Department of Sociology, California State University, Hayward, California, 1978.

11. Ann Oakley, *Woman's Work: The Housewife Past and Present,* New York, Vintage, 1976, p. 234.

12. Edward Pohlman, *The Psychology of Birth Planning,* Cambridge, Schenkman, 1969, p. 172.

13. For a discussion of several studies dealing with parenthood as a "crisis," see: Alice S. Rossi, "Transition to Parenthood." *Journal of Marriage and the Family,* 1968, Vol. 30.

14. Sandra L. Hofferth and Kristin A. Moore, "Early Childbearing and Later Economic Well Being," *American Sociological Review,* 1979, Vol. 44, p. 809. For

further information on family employment patterns, see: George Masnick and Mary Jo Bane, *The Nation's Families 1960–1990*. Cambridge, Joint Center for Urban Studies of MIT and Harvard University, 1980.

Chapter Six

1. John Peel and Griselda Carr, *Contraception And Family Design,* Edingburg: Churchill-Livingston, 1975, p. 31.
2. Levinson, op. cit., p. 73.
3. Robert Gunther, ''Young People are Pessimistic About Ever Affording a Home,'' *Wall Street Journal,* February 17, 1982, p. 27.
4. Gunther, ibid., p. 27.
5. Elliot Currie, Robert Dunn and David Fogarty, ''The New Immiseration; Stagflation, Inequality, and the Working Class,'' *Socialist Review* Vol. 54 1981, p. 20.
6. See for example: Michael P. Fogarty, Rhona Rapoport and Robert N. Rapoport, *Sex, Career And Family,* London: George Allen & Unwin Ltd., 1971, and Caroline Bird, *The Two-Paycheck Family,* New York: Simon & Schuster.
7. Leonard Benson, *Fatherhood: A Sociological Perspective,* New York: Random House, 1968, p. 127.
8. Ellen Ross ''The Love Crisis: Couple's Advice Books of the Late 1970's,'' *Signs: Journal of Woman in Culture and Society,* Vol. 6, no. 1, 1980.
9. Marilyn Fabe and Norma Winkler, *Up Against the Clock: Career Women Speak on the Choice to Have Children,* New York: Random House, 1979, p. 132.
10. Lewis J. Ford, ''Delayed Baby Boom: Its Meaning'', *U.S. News and World Report,* February 20, 1978, p. 41. Elsewhere Westhoff predicts that voluntary childless marriages are greatly increasing: ''If current rates for first births were to persist, some 30% of U.S. women now of child bearing age would never have any children.'' Charles F. Westhoff, ''Marriage and Fertility in the Developing Countries.'' *Scientific American,* Vol. 239, No. 6, 1978, p. 55.
11. See, for example: J. E. Veevers, ''Voluntarily Childless Wives; An Exploratory Study,'' *Sociology and Social Research,* Vol. 57, 1973, pp. 356–366.
12. U.S. Bureau of the Census, Current Population reports, ''Trends in Childspacing, June 1975,'' (Washington D.C.: U.S. Printing Office, 1978.)
13. Major studies which report a shift towards postponed parenthood are those of Ross Stolzenberg and Linda J. Waite, ''Age, Fertility Expectations and Plans for Employment,'' *Amer. Sociological Review,* Vol. 42, 1977, pp. 769–783, and George Masnick and Mary Jo Bane *The Nations Families: 1960–1990.* Cambridge: Joint Center for Urban Studies of M.I.T. and Harvard Univ. 1980.

Chapter Seven

1. Jean E. Veevers, ''The Life Style of Voluntarily Childless Couples,'' London, Ontario, Canada (Mimeographed), 1974, p. 1.

2. U.S. Bureau of the Census, *Population Profile of the United States, 1977,''* Washington D.C.: U.S. Government Printing Office, 1978, p. 3.

3. Karen S. Renne, "Childlessness, Health and Marital Satisfaction," *Social Biology,* Vol. 23, 1978, p. 188.

4. Ellen Peck, *The Baby Trap,* New York, Geis and Associates, 1972.; Anna and Arnold Silverman, *The Case Against Having Children,* New York, David McKay, 1971.; Elizabeth M. Whelan, M.D., *A Baby? . . . Maybe,* New York, Bobbs-Merrill, 1975.

5. Marjorie R. Leonard, "Fathers and Daughters: The Significance of 'Fathering' in the Psychosexual Development of the Girl," *International Journal of Psychoanalysis,* Vol. 47, (1966), p. 329. Also see: Robert J. Stoller, "The Sense of Femaleness," *Psychoanalytic Quarterly* Vol. 37, 1968, pp. 42–55. E. M. Hetherington, "Effects of Father Absence on Personality Development in Adolescent Daughters," *Developmental Psychology,* Vol. 7, 1972, pp. 313–326, and Alfred B. Heilbrun, Jr., "Identification with the Father and Sex-Role Development of the Daughter," *The Family Coordinator,* Vol. 25, 1976, pp. 411–415.

6. Herbert Marshall McLuhan, *The Mechanical Bride: Folklore of Industrial Man,* Boston, Beacon Press, 1967, p. 68.

7. William Reynolds, *The American Father,* New York, Paddington Press, Ltd., 1968, pp. 25–27.

8. Jean E. Veevers, "The Childfree Alternative: Rejection of the Motherhood Mystique" in *Woman in Canada,* Marylee Stephenson (ed.), Toronto, New Press, 1973, p. 187.

9. Andrew Hacker, "Farewell to the Family," *New York Times Review of Books,* March 18, 1982, p. 41.

10. Edward Pohlman, "Childlessness: Intentional and Unintentional, Psychological and Social Aspects," *Journal of Nervous and Mental Diseases,* Vol. 151, 1970, p. 9.

11. Angus Campbell, "The American Way of Mating: Marriage, Si; Children, Only Maybe," *Psychology Today,* 1975, p. 39.

12. Sharon K. Houseknecht, "Childlessness and Marital Adjustment," *Journal of Marriage and the Family,* 1979, p. 262.

13. Houseknecht, ibid, p. 263.

14. Renne, op. cit., p. 196.

15. Shirley Radl, *Mother's Day Is Over,* New York, Warner Books, 1973, p. 52.

16. Ellen Peck, "Television's Romance with Reproduction," in Ellen Peck and Judith Senderowitz (editors), *Pronatalism: The Myth of Man and Apple Pie,* New York: Thomas Cromwell, 1974, pp. 84–85.

17. Pohlman, op. cit., p. 5.

18. Peck, op. cit., p. 61.

19. Peck, ibid, p. 37.

20. Betty Rollin, "Motherhood: Who Needs It?", *Look,* Oct. 22, 1970, p. 17.

21. Gael Green, "A Vote Against Motherhood" in Peck and Senderowitz, op. cit., p. 268.

22. Ellen M. Nason and Margaret M. Paloma, *Voluntarily Childless Couples: The Emergence of a Variant Lifestyle,* Beverly Hills, Sage Publications, 1976, p. 21.

23. Veevers in Stephenson, op. cit., p. 192–193.

24. Patricia Crane, "Processes Surrounding a Decision to Remain Childless," a paper presented at the Pacific Sociological Association meetings, Spokane, Washington, 1978, p. 28.

25. Charles F. Westhoff, "Marriage and Fertility in the Developed Countries," *Scientific American,* Vol. 239, December, 1978, p. 55.

Chapter Eight

1. Erich Fromm, *The Art of Loving,* New York, Harper and Row, Publishers, 1974, p. 86.

2. Diane Vaughn, *Uncoupling: Turning Points in Intimate Relationships,* New York, Oxford University Press, 1986.

Self-Study Projects

We have included four SELF-STUDY PROJECTS at the end of the book. The purpose of these projects is to try to gain a better understanding of your important relationships. Therefore it is very important that you respond as openly as possible. The project pages are perforated so that each one can be removed.

We have also included a list of study questions prepared by our colleague, Professor Diane R. Beeson.

FIRST PROJECT: GETTING CLEAR

Please describe your personal (nonacademic) reasons for taking this course. What of personal value do you hope to get out of it? What relationship(s) do you hope to handle better?

SECOND PROJECT: DESCRIBING 'LOVE OBJECTS'

1. Using only adjectives, describe yourself.
2. Using only adjectives, describe your opposite sex parent.
3. Using only adjectives, describe the person that you are now closely involved with.
4. Using only adjectives, describe your ideal mate.

THIRD PROJECT: MANAGING CONFLICT

Please describe what you and your lover or mate disagree about. It other words, what are your typical arguments about? How do each of you handle these disagreements?

FOURTH PROJECT: MOVING FORWARD

1. Of the three timetables, which do you prefer and why?
2. Which timetable does your (actual or potential) mate prefer?
3. If they are different, how would you try to reconcile them?

STUDY QUESTIONS

1. What are three recent historical changes that have radically changed the conditions of marriage and family life according to the authors?
2. What were the five basic criteria all of the newlyweds had to meet before they were selected to be interviewed?
3. What proportion of the newlyweds followed the traditional path to matrimony?
4. What differences did the authors find between cohabitors and the traditionally engaged couple?
5. To what extent did cohabitors experience pressure to marry?
6. Why do the authors call the process that occurs during the first year the spectre of sexual burnout?
7. What was the most formidable challenge of the first year?
8. What happens to existing friendships during the first year?
9. What new perspective on intimacy emerged during the second year?
10. What are the three phases newlyweds move through by the end of the second year?
11. How did early nester men view marriage?
12. What did early nester women expect from their husbands?
13. What are the characteristics of families of origin of early nesters?
14. What was the highest priority for postponers?
15. How did the postponer's timetable change over time?
16. In what ways were childfree couples similar to postponers?
17. How is refusal to have a child often viewed?
18. What fear did several newlyweds express about the arrival of a child?
19. First year couples had an opportunity to convert romance into what?
20. What benefits do effective timetables provide a couple?